T
REAL YOU
BELIEVING YOUR TRUE IDENTITY

LINDA BREITMAN
FOREWORDS BY GRAHAM COOKE & BILL YOUNT

The Real You - Believing Your True Identity
Published by Linda Breitman Ministries.
© 2013 by Linda Breitman

Printed in the United States of America
ISBN-10: 0989411303
ISBN-13: 978-0-9894113-0-1

For information contact:
Linda Breitman Ministries
LindaBreitman.com

I DEDICATE THIS BOOK TO MY BELOVED MOTHER WHO ALWAYS BELIEVED IN ME.

I ALSO DEDICATE THIS BOOK TO MY WONDERFUL HUSBAND—KING TURKEY—WHO CONSTANTLY HAS MY BACK SPIRITUALLY AND GRAMMATICALLY! I LOVE YOU! QUACK!

ACKNOWLEDGMENTS

I would like to acknowledge Lauren Gallaway for overseeing the entire Real You project. Your great ideas and hard work have been invaluable. You've overcome so many challenges and are always positive. You carry not only the favor of God but also the joy of the Lord. We have been on an exciting journey together—with each day bringing more fun. So many days I've felt like we have boldly gone where no man has been before! Yay!

I am grateful for all the hours my dear husband Les invested in editing. You are brilliant. You make me look good! Quack!

Joanne Stroud, thank you for your on-going intercession for this project. You have persevered with me for the past few years and helped me finally deliver this baby. I am deeply grateful for how you continually imparted wisdom and encouragement.

Debra Hogervorst is a gifted director, producer, cinematographer, and editor. I appreciate your creativity and dedication. The teaching videos came out great—very down-to-earth and authentic. I so appreciate our friendship.

Thanks to Kat Flippin for extensive research, proofreading, and handling so many details. You are a joy.

Thanks to all those who prayed, encouraged and supported me in some way—John and Judy Ross, Nate Firth, Steven Anderson, Jim and Julia Pinzenscham, Tom McGurin, Mike Hubbard, Annette Moreno, Aaron Jayne, Bob Cathers, and Bill Yount. I would like to thank the girls, my beautiful spiritual daughters. You have been an inspiration to me. All our years together have more fully formed the revelation on identity. There are so many more I would like to thank. I have been blessed with so many amazing friends. Thank you all.

ENDORSEMENTS

Change doesn't begin around you until it is identified within you. Your mind is the birthplace for your feelings, your function, and your future realities. In this magnificent book, Linda Breitman has opened the door for unlimited miracles to fill your life as you begin to understand your new identity in Christ. Step-by-step you will journey into a profound comprehension of God's overwhelmingly good thoughts toward you. Once you have saturated in the wealth of revelation found within the pages of this gem, you will unmistakingly know that you are accepted, valued, and chosen by God. This book will help to bring a paradigm shift into your mind... that will overflow into your life. Get ready to receive the change that you've prayed for... read this book and you will be blessed!

JOSHUA MILLS
International Conference Speaker and Best-selling Author "31 Days To A Miracle Mindset"
Vancouver, BC, Canada
www.JoshuaMills.com

As blood-bought, Spirit-filled believers, we have a mandate to release the Kingdom of Heaven into the earthly realm—loosing miracles, prosperity, restoration of families, and the very blueprints of heaven. We are the "doors" and "gates" of the supernatural—the very conduits through whom heaven touches earth. For some, however, after the born again experience occurs, these pathways and mental faculties never fully open to the reality of the supernatural that comes from the renewal of the mind and living from our new heavenly identity. In her book, Linda Breitman releases not only the truth of your new nature in Christ but provides high level activation exercises to renew your mind according to the Word of God, allowing the supernatural to flow as you begin living as the real you. Read it. Apply it. Live it.

JEFF JANSEN
Founder, Global Fire Ministries International
Global Fire Church & World Miracle Center
Kingdom Life Institute
Author, Glory Rising & Furious Sound of Glory
www.globalfireministries.com

These are days of consummation, fullness, and harvest. Clearly all seeds sown into the earth are coming to maturity simultaneously. The sons of the Kingdom must respond to this call by understanding who they are in Christ and the potential He imparts to us. As we learn to posture ourselves in perfect alignment with heaven, the flow of the Lord's nature and ability will find its resting place in us. Linda Breitman has captured the essence of that mandate and provided incredible tools to help us fulfill our destiny and purpose. The biblical truths and practical applications you'll discover in this book will prove invaluable in your pursuit of the Lord and personal destiny. It is for that purpose that I recommend *The Real You: Believing Your True Identity* to any believer hungry for God and the fullness of His purposes.

PAUL KEITH DAVIS
WhiteDove Ministries

Linda Breitman is a friend, leader, and mentor of many. She has a lifetime of experience in the realm of identity. This long awaited book will greatly add to the important field of knowing our identity in Christ. Finally, as you read this book, the real you can come to the surface.

JONATHAN WELTON
Best-Selling Author & Director of The Welton Academy

Ministry schools, leaders, and Bible study teachers all need this book! It is an identity transformer! People want to operate in the supernatural, but mental strongholds stop them in their tracks. Negative self-talk sabotages people—especially young people who are passionate about God. I have known Linda for fifteen years, and as Senior Pastor of an apostolic training center, I highly recommend her ministry. She is very prophetic and gifted. *The Real You* is an effective identity training guide.

JOHN ROSS
Senior Pastor and Apostolic Leader of Cloud Nine Worship Center
San Diego, California

Linda's book helps us to listen to the correct inner tapes of who we really are and what God's destiny is for us. You will never feel comfortable in your own skin until you realize how God has made you, your giftings, your passion, your design. This book is critical to that process. Read it, walk through it, and watch as your identity crisis gets unpeeled and unwrapped and the real you stands up.

GARY GOODELL
Third Day Churches, Inc.
Author of, "Permission Granted To Do Church Differently in the 21st Century," and "Where Would Jesus Lead?"

CONTENTS

FOREWORDS

Transformation is based on our identity in Jesus not on our behavior, which is always changing as the refining process and the consequential upgrades continue to impart deeper truth and life to our relationship with the Lord. Identity provides us with a solid base with which to explore the fullness of God's intention and affection for us in Christ Jesus. We are learning to be overwhelmed by His goodness and kindness, which graces us with the beauty of who God wants to be for us in any given situation.

It is normal for us, when confronted by the sheer elegance of the love of God, to want to know how He perceives and thinks of us on a personal level. We are the new man in Christ. That is our identity! We are not the old man of sin that has been done away with on the cross of Jesus. He did not just die for us, but He wonderfully and providentially died as us, thus releasing us to a newness of life (Romans 6:4) where we are learning to become occupied (fully alive) with God as beloved children who are developing into fully mature sons in the faith. What an adventure! Our story and our journey are transformed when we know how we are loved and viewed by the Father.

Many believers want new but think old. Others are trapped by a religious system that majors on the old man, is obsessed by sin and preaches behavior modification in a weird kind of self-help program that can only produce a present past lifestyle and is inherently wearisome and powerless.

Our DNA in Christ has a partner gene because of His wonderful relationship with the Holy Spirit. We are being made into His image because our Helper in God, the incomparable Holy Spirit, delights in taking everything that belongs to Jesus and making it real for us in daily life (John 16). The Spirit steps into our weak places in a very timely and intentional manner to support us in the process of becoming ever more confident and mature in our connections with the Father (Romans 8:26, 28).

I love the posture element of Linda's book. It reminds me so much of the absolute joy that the Holy Spirit has in posturing Himself into our life events. If we are in Christ, then so are all our circumstances! If we cannot be separated from God's love (Romans 8:33-39) then our circumstances can never be separated from God's intention toward us. Posturing before Him in the Word is a solid part of our learning to abide in Jesus.

The only undiscovered country for Christians to explore is the territory between their ears! Learning how to think with the mind of Christ is vital. Being renewed in the spirit of our minds is essential (Ephesians 4:20-24). Learning how to spiritually appraise (1 Corinthians 2:12-16) our areas of difficulty and problematic situations is part of our joyful journey in Christ (James 1:2-5; 1 Thessalonians 5:16-18).

God does not call us on our behavior since the old man is dead. He calls us up to our identity in Christ as free men (Romans 6:7, Galatians 2:20). Jesus said, "My sheep know My voice"; therefore, we must in all areas of life discover and embrace those words that the Lord is constructively speaking to us. If that is not our regular practice, we will default to words of destruction in critical moments. Who and what is building us up, and who/ what is pulling us down? Choose wisely.

Taking charge of our thought lives is vital. Learn to examine the issues of life in the context of what God wants to be for you in this moment. This is where Linda's book is so valuable. *The Real*

You provides us with valuable keys that empower us to discover the mind of the Lord. We are learning how His dominant thinking can govern our life issues, making us vulnerable to His goodness and kindness.

If we think negatively, we become negative. Life in Christ, however, is so much more powerful than mere positive thinking. God has the only accurate picture of who we really are...its called Scripture, and we all find our identity in it. The world always provides us with negative information; therefore, we cannot take our cues from the natural world. We are not earthbound in our thinking because the mind of Christ sets us in a place far above all that the world can see and process.

Our own process is more spiritual, more dynamic, wisdom based, and relational with the Lord. We are in the process of learning what God sees when He looks at us. That learning must actively replace all other perceptions. Then we must develop the joy and peace in believing His perspective. We confess our identity for all that He is worth!!

When we embrace the whole truth about our identity, we can learn to be over-comers in all our life events. Identity is the key issue in our relationship with God. It is the area where the enemy deploys lots of resources against us and is, therefore, also the biggest area of dynamic favor from the Lord. Brilliant. Crisis is where lordship is made visible. We can know the truth in our heads but not allow it to grow within to the place where it radically affects thinking, perception, language, and belief. Truth is always acted out in life. It is in our partnership with the Holy Spirit where the truth of Jesus sets us free.

I love the wealth of Scripture, the posturing element, and the decrees that are all made possible in the Holy Spirit. This is where *The Real You* can make an incredible difference to your walk with

God. How we are known in heaven is essential understanding in the unfolding of identity. All of heaven is attracted to Jesus in us!

This book is an excellent tool for young believers and also for established Christians who need refreshing in identity thinking or perhaps need to reinvent who they are becoming in the Kingdom. This book contains a very good step-by-step guide to get us thinking, talking, seeing, and believing something better about ourselves.

The Real You is an excellent resource as a mentoring, small group, or training course in the local church or Christian organization. It will provoke a wonderful dialogue and impact on our spiritual growth to upgrade us in our relationship with the Lord Jesus.

GRAHAM COOKE
Author, speaker, consultant
www.brilliantperspectives.com

Imagine yourself in the shoes of Nik Wallenda of the famed "Flying Wallendas," walking a tight rope over the Grand Canyon. There is no safety net. Dreadful questions begin to arise. "What were you thinking? Who do you think you are, challenging the forces of nature?"

At 1500 feet above the canyon, these thoughts couldn't stop you. You remained focused on walking out your lifelong dream. With each step, the one dominating thought seeded in your mind years ago absolutely girded your feet to the two inch high wire. You were walking out your thoughts. "I *can* do this. I can do *all* things through Christ who strengthens me" (Philippians 4:13).

The first thought that conceived your historic dream came with doubts flooding your mind. But you stood your ground. You knew you were always just one thought away from fulfilling your destiny. That dream was from God. He believes in you. You began to prepare in the natural by training on tight ropes under violent weather patterns—patterns you would likely face during this outrageous event. You refused to give negative thoughts any entrance into your mind. Your thoughts would take you over the Grand Canyon a thousand times before your feet ever touched the actual high wire.

What about you? What are you thinking? Who do you *think* you are? Do you have limiting mindsets, or do you think you can do all things through Christ? Before God spoke the world into existence, He thought about it. Before God created you, *you* were in His thoughts. He thought you up! "Before I formed you in the womb I knew you, before you were born I set you apart" (Jeremiah 1:5). He loved you perfectly before you were conceived. *You* are His dream come true. And you were then born to create your own dream.

What thought will cause you to walk out your dream as the world looks on and wonders, "Who do you think you are?"

Linda Breitman, a woman of integrity and known to be dangerous to the powers of darkness, has spoken at strategic times into my life, bringing major breakthroughs and encouragement. She has trained many to come into their identity in Christ to fulfill their outrageous dreams. Linda's book, *The Real You, Believing Your True Identity*, is a powerful training guide heaven sent for this hour. Read and study it as you walk the tight rope of your dreams.

BILL YOUNT
Author of I Heard Heaven Proclaim and Prophetic Stones of Remembrance
Blowing the Shofar Ministries
www.billyount.com

INTRODUCTION

There is a pure and spotless Bride living inside of you. Loyal and beloved.

There is a warrior living inside of you. Tenacious and true.

There is a lover living inside of you. Intimate and pure.

Your full identity is living inside of you. The identity God gave you. The Real You.

You are royalty. You are kings and priests, princes and princesses—destined to reflect God's glory. Knowing your identity cultivates your prophetic destiny. Your prophetic destiny is unique to you. You have dreams and visions and talents—ready to blossom forth in your life. *The Real You* calls forth your true identity and trains you to align your thoughts with heaven so you can move on toward fulfilling your prophetic destiny.

LINDA BREITMAN
May 2013

1

Finally, brothers, whatever is true, whatever is noble, whatever is right, whatever is pure, whatever is lovely, whatever is admirable—if anything is excellent or praiseworthy—think about such things.

PHILIPPIANS 4:8

ALIGN YOUR THOUGHTS WITH HEAVEN

Think: To carefully reflect on.

If I could crawl inside your mind for twenty-four hours, would I have a good day? Whenever I ask that question, most people have the same response—shock. Their jaws drop open, and their eyes get real big. Imagine someone being able to listen in on your thoughts. Yikes! What a disaster!

We are brilliant at making ourselves look good on the outside while privately our minds are telling us something entirely different—something negative and limiting. Deep in our hearts, we long to embrace God's destiny for us and to know our true identity. We want to be more like Jesus. And yes, we desire to do supernatural exploits that defy this natural world. It is in our spiritual DNA to enter God's world and partner with Him, but our minds *fight* us—and the demonic realm opposes us. There is a war going on, and long ago God designated the winner—*you*. Your part is to cooperate with God by believing your *true identity*. Where do you begin? Right between your ears—with your thoughts.

At the most unexpected times, a threatening, insidious voice rears its ugly head and tries to steal your dreams: *You can't do this. You don't know how. You'll never succeed. You're not smart enough. You're not pretty enough. Who do you think you are, anyway?* Any of this sound familiar? Maybe these thoughts are not in the forefront of your thinking. Maybe you have squashed some of them down. But all of us have fought with the voices of opposition that endeavor to suck the life out of our plans when we dream big.

The Holy Spirit downloads ideas and dreams into our spirits. He *loves* for us to dream big. He speaks to us of our true identity. He stirs up places of creativity within us and then pours in strategies so we can really attain our aspirations. Yet most of our precious dreams go unrealized. Why? *Because our self-talk negates them.* We argue with the inner pictures implanted by the Holy Spirit, and a negative mindset short-circuits His plans. We defeat the images He places in our minds when we take no definite action to align our thoughts with the mind of Christ. This is a key: You uncover the *real* you when you align your *mind* with God's perception of you.

The mind is a war zone—a battlefield—where thoughts constantly fight each other for supremacy. This battle rages daily, with your dominant thoughts winning and ruling your life. For example, if you think depressing thoughts, you get depressed. If you think God's thoughts of you, you feel encouraged. You can think yourself into a rotten mood. You can think yourself into a happy mood. Consider what you think about: Do your most dominant thoughts depict an accurate picture of who God says you are?

For years, mine did not. I didn't even know what an accurate picture of myself looked like. If I could change my inner thought life, into what kinds of thoughts would I change them? How would I do it? Once I entered into a life of walking with Jesus, the Holy Spirit began leading me into a new world of thought—a world of thinking outrageous, supernatural God thoughts. I needed to stop thinking the way the world thought and to embark on a journey of rewiring my mind and being completely transformed to *align my thoughts with heaven.*

God specifically calls this process *renewing* our minds:

Do not conform any longer to the pattern of this world, but ***be transformed by the renewing of your mind.*** *Then you will be able to test and approve what God's will is—His good, pleasing and perfect will* (Romans 12:2).

Who does the renewing? *We* do. We take deliberate action to pull out a lifetime of wrong, negative thoughts and replace them with what God says is true about us. If it sounds aggressive, it is. A real renewed mind blows the lid off limited thinking. We try to figure things out according to how the world operates. A real renewed mind is not earthbound in its thinking. A renewed mind is tapped into the mind of Christ—God's way of seeing things. You start this renewing process by pulling down wrong mindsets.

Check this out:

We demolish arguments and every pretension that sets itself up against the knowledge of God, and we ***take captive every thought*** *to make it obedient to Christ* (2 Corinthians 10:5).

Every thought contrary to God's truth can be demolished, destroyed, and replaced with what is true.

When we renew our minds, we are simply cooperating with God, and an incredible, supernatural transformation begins, which leads us right into living our lives in the supernatural power of God—with signs and wonders following us.

Does this transformation happen quickly? Sometimes a light bulb goes on when you learn a new aspect of your identity and you have an "Aha!" moment, but most of the time it is a gradual process. Aligning your mind with heaven is a daily choice, and as long as you are living on planet earth, you are never done. Know one thing for sure: You do *not* have to accept every thought that comes drifting along, trying to implant itself in your mind. You can *refuse* thoughts. You can say, "I'm not going to think that. I'm going to think...." And make a conscious choice to think from God's viewpoint. By posturing with God's Word, you are purposefully re-wiring your thinking by praying and declaring reality from heaven's perspective.

The purpose of this book is to help you begin building up the real you by looking deeply at what Scripture says about how you think and what you think. It is the battle for your *mind*. You have probably said, "God, I want to see miracles. I want a supernatural lifestyle! I want to engage with You, partner with You, and experience You!" Well, my friend, the mind is the gateway to the supernatural. You may not have realized how much of the Bible addresses your thoughts. As you declare these personalized verses about your thought life, you will be breaking agreements with lies and confronting the spirit realm. You will begin planting, building, and establishing powerful mindsets— mindsets taken directly from Scripture. You will begin posturing for a transformed life.

I urge you to grasp the strength of each truth. Be aggressive. Speak the following verses out loud. Say each verse with feeling and confidence. Feel yourself being transformed. The way to becoming dangerous men and women of God is to *agree* with God. When you agree with Him, you uncover your true identity. Advance the Kingdom of God in your life and take new ground! Hoo-ah!

Pray Before You Posture

God, help me see the truth about what I am speaking.
Breathe life on my proclamations and break off past thought
patterns that are contrary to Your truth, in Jesus' name.

Posturing: Taking Charge of My Thoughts

The mind is a battlefield. The battle is for my thought-life. (2 Cor. 10:3-5)

I demolish every thought not in agreement with what God says about me. (2 Cor. 10:3-5)

I take captive every thought and make it obedient to Christ. (2 Cor. 10:3-5)

I am fighting this battle, and I am winning. (2 Cor. 10:3-5)

I choose to believe God and trust God by speaking words of life and hope and truth. (2 Cor. 10:3-5)

When it comes to my thought life, I am a warrior. I put on the full armor of God. (Eph. 6:11-17)

My sword is the sword of the Spirit, which is the Word of God. (Eph. 6:11-17)

I speak forth the Word of God with clarity and boldness, hitting targets right and left, long before they can set up camp in my mind. (2 COR. 10:3-5)

I am not ignorant of the devil's devices. I am alert and my guard is up. (1 PET. 5:8)

Though he may try to plant thoughts and images in my mind, I do not entertain them. (1 PET. 5:8)

I know he prowls around like a lion, looking for whom he may devour. And it's not going to be me. (1 PET. 5:8-9)

I resist him, standing firm in my faith. (1 PET. 5:9)

I am on the lookout for any thoughts that are in opposition to God. (2 COR. 10:5)

I am determined to be victorious in the battle for my mind. (2 COR. 10:5)

I purposely dismantle and destroy destructive thoughts and replace them with the truth of who I am. (2 COR. 10:5)

I do not conform any longer to the pattern of this world, but I am transformed by the renewing of my mind. (ROM. 12:2)

I understand that death and life are in the power of the tongue. (PROV. 18:21)

Words kill; words give life. Thoughts kill; thoughts give life. (PROV. 18:21)

I choose life. (PROV. 18:21)

I make myself aware of the thoughts in my mind so that the words I speak are words of life. (PROV. 18:21)

I gird up the loins of my mind. (1 PET. 1:13)

That means I prepare my mind for action. I am alert and thinking clearly. (1 PET. 1:13)

I focus my inner thought life on that which is true and honorable and right and pure and lovely and admirable—things that are excellent and worthy of praise. (PHIL. 4:8)

I have the mind of Christ. (1 COR. 2:16)

God keeps me in perfect peace because my mind is steadfast, trusting in Him. (ISA. 26:3)

I am constantly renewed in the spirit of my mind. (EPH. 4:23)

I am being renewed in my thoughts and attitudes. (EPH. 4:23)

I am being transformed into an entirely new way of life—a God-designed life. (EPH. 4:23)

A deep inner change is happening to me. (EPH. 4:23)

I am being renewed on the inside, and it is working itself to the outside as God reproduces His character in me. (EPH. 4:23)

How do I keep my way pure? By living according to Your Word. (PS. 119:9)

With my lips I declare the counsel that comes from Your mouth. (PS. 119:13)

To be spiritually minded is life and peace. (ROM. 8:6)

In the presence of God, I meditate on His unfailing love. (PS. 48:9)

God has not given me a spirit of fear, but of power and love and a sound mind. (2 TIM. 1:7)

I serve You, Lord, with wholehearted devotion and a willing mind. (1 CHRON. 28:9)

You search my heart and understand every motive behind my thoughts. (1 CHRON. 28:9)

I love You, Lord, with all my heart, and with all my soul, and with all my mind. (MATT. 22:37)

I set my mind on things that are above, not on things that are on the earth. (COL. 3:2)

Lord, I position my mind to see things from Your perspective. (COL. 3:2)

On my bed I remember You. My thoughts are of You through the watches of the night. (Ps. 63:6)

May the words of my mouth and the quiet meditations of my heart be pleasing to You, Lord. (Ps. 19:14)

My mind is focused on what the Spirit desires. I choose to seek after things the Spirit desires. (ROM. 8:5)

Your Word is living and active. (HEB. 4:12)

Sharper than any double-edged sword, it penetrates even to dividing soul and spirit, joints and marrow. (HEB. 4:12)

It exposes the very thoughts and attitudes of my heart. (HEB. 4:12)

I meditate on Your Word day and night. (Ps. 1:2)

I delight in Your words. (Ps. 1:2)

I posture my thoughts in the truth of Your Word. (Ps. 1:2)

IDENTITY ACTIVATIONS: NEW MINDSETS

ONE. Renewing your mind by posturing in the Word of God establishes and builds your real identity. In the first activation, you will begin learning how to *posture*. To posture is to position yourself. It means you are taking a specific stance. When you posture in God's Word, you position yourself to be in agreement with God. You are no longer aligning yourself with worldly thinking, but rather you are aligning yourself with God's perspective. It is vital that your deep inner dialog reflects God's Word. You are *not* exchanging one earthbound mindset for another earthbound mindset. When you speak God's Word, you are stepping into agreement with heaven. Take the posturing verses you just read and incorporate them into your daily life. *You* are the one who renews your mind. *You* take up the sword of the Spirit which is the Word of God and proclaim it. This is a week-long activation—and it is the most powerful of all. If you do nothing else—*posture*.

> *Whatever controls your thoughts, controls you.*

Your assignment is this: Read the verses first thing in the morning when you get up and right before you go to bed. Decide right now you are going to make this your priority. Carry the verses with you and speak them throughout the day. There is no such thing as proclaiming God's Word too much. I will tell you right now that you will be challenged to give up, quit, or simply forget. Recognize the warfare. All the forces of hell are at work to prevent you from speaking verses that build your true identity. It takes effort and perseverance. Dig down deep and tap into a warrior mindset! Always remember that you are in a war. And the battle is for your mind!

Two. As you posture, you may find difficulty fully believing and even speaking some of the verses. When this happens, you most likely have believed a lie. A lie is a wrong mindset. The lie will pretty much be the opposite of your proclamation. This is a place in your mind that needs to be *renewed*. Choose a verse that you are having a hard time fully believing. Write the verse. Now, ask the Holy Spirit: "What is the lie I accepted as truth that kept me from believing this verse?" Write down the lie the Holy Spirit shows you. Maybe you have believed you can't change the way you think or that you just automatically think negative thoughts. Or you still believe negative things someone said to you.

Ask God to forgive you for believing the lie. Verbally break the agreement you have had with the lie. For example, you can say, "Lord, I am sorry for believing the lie. It kept me from believing Your Word. In Jesus' name, I break my agreement with that lie. Now, I believe _____." Write the verse again in your own words. You have begun demolishing a stronghold. You are replacing wrong mindsets with mindsets that truly reflect your identity.

Often, there is an injured place in our hearts where the lie came in. You don't have to even identify the injury for God to heal your heart. Just ask Him to heal you. Say, "Lord, heal the injured place in my heart where the lie came in."

Sit quietly for a moment. The Holy Spirit is healing your heart and mind. You are purposefully pulling down a worldly or demonic stronghold and planting truth in its place. As you do, you will begin feeling differently about the verses with which you previously struggled. Apply this process with any hard-to-accept verse. Demolishing strongholds requires a conscious effort on your part, but you can do this. God has created you to be an overcomer.

THREE This Identity Activation is important, and many skip over it. Don't. Get a few sheets of paper, set a timer, and for five minutes, write whatever comes to mind. Write your thoughts without stopping. Write the positive things you say to yourself as well as the negative things. Take a look. Writing your thoughts will give you an indication as to what you tend to think about when you're not really thinking about what you're thinking.

FOUR. Look up 2 Corinthians 10:3-5 in a few different translations. What is the Holy Spirit revealing to you through this passage?

FIVE. Draw a picture of a person with a renewed mind and another picture of a person with old mindsets. Draw how each person looks on the outside and on the inside. What do you see? Which one reflects the *real* you?

PRAYER: TRANSFORMING MY THOUGHT LIFE

Dear Lord,

   My thoughts bear fruit. I am purposefully choosing to take up my sword, and I am cutting out thoughts that are contrary to You. I am seated in heavenly realms, and I am postured in heavenly realms. I am actively renewing my mind and viewing reality from Your perspective. Help me to think about what I'm thinking about so that my thoughts bear good, positive fruit.

Amen

HEAVENLY WORD

Beloved, your mind is the gateway to a supernatural life with Me. Fully believe you are seated in heavenly realms—because you are. Right now! Posture yourself in heavenly realms by aligning your thoughts with Mine. What you think about Me and about yourself carries a lot of weight. Strengthen your mind. Death and life are in the power of the tongue. You eat the fruit of what you say. Speak Life!

ROMANS 12:2; EPHESIANS 2:6; 1 PETER 1:13; PROVERBS 18:21

2

*Do not conform any longer to the pattern of this world,
but be transformed by the renewing of your mind. Then
you will be able to test and approve what God's will
is—his good, pleasing and perfect will.*

ROMANS 12:2

YOUR NEW IDENTITY

Renew: The adjustment of the moral and spiritual vision and thinking to the mind of God, which is designed to have a transforming effect upon the life[1]

Did you ever wonder, "Who am I? Where am I going? What's the meaning of life?" I did. "What is the purpose of my life? What should I do with my life?" Like most young people, I wanted to find significance to my life. I wanted to *do* something significant. I wanted to *feel* significant. My personal identity changed with the wind. When I was studying at the university, I identified myself as a student. When I was married, I was a wife. When I was in a play, I was an actress. I identified myself with whatever job I had. I based my identity on something outside of my self—something from the world. I defined my identity by specific criteria: what I did and what I had. Nothing else. Until Jesus.

Everything we say and do is influenced by how we see ourselves. That's identity—how we see ourselves. With a brand new budding relationship with Christ, my accomplishments were no longer the basis for my worth. A giant paradigm shift in my self-perception ensued as I looked to God for answers. Seeing myself through God's eyes was a beautiful view. Nonetheless, I was challenged daily as old beliefs slapped me in the face. To grow solid in my real identity, I knew I had to learn what God said about me, and then I needed to *believe* it. The only way to do this was to read His book and discover for myself what He said about my identity. As a new creation in Christ, I had a new identity to embrace. And so do you.

The most significant battle in your Christian walk is the one for your spiritual identity. Every other battle hinges on it. The devil does not want you to believe who you are. Oh sure, you can know *about* God and all the mind-boggling truths He says about you. But the devil does not want you to *believe* it. And act on it. And speak it. Because then you would become really dangerous. You would begin leading people to Christ, healing the sick, casting out demons, and changing the world.

Before Jesus carried out His life mission, the Holy Spirit led Him into the wilderness where satan challenged Him. He said to Jesus,

> **If you are the Son of God**, *tell this stone to become bread* (Luke 4:3).

> *"If you are the Son of God,"* he said, *"throw yourself down from here. For it is written: 'He will command his angels concerning you to guard you carefully...'"* (Luke 4:9-10).

As satan repeatedly challenged Jesus' identity, His responses to the accusations were consistent: "It is *written!* It is *written!* It is *written!*" Jesus countered demonic accusations by proclaiming the truth and authority of the written Word. He repeated what God the Father had long stated as undeniable, irrevocable truth. Right here is a very important fact for you to remember about spiritual warfare: If Jesus was challenged on His identity, you can be assured that you will be challenged on your identity as well. Every day. As you grow in the renewing of your mind and continue tearing down old mental strongholds, your response will become second nature as you adamantly proclaim, "It is *written!*"

Jesus always referred to the authority of Scripture. As you follow His lead, decreeing your identity from Scripture, tremendous authority will rise up inside you, and you will embrace who you really are—the real you. Your real identity. Knowing your identity and believing it greatly impacts the way your destiny unfolds. You *are* a man, a woman of destiny!

The *you* God meant for you to be is bold and confident and tender and strong. The real you is stunningly courageous. The real you is wildly loved. You have gifts and abilities from God, and He wants you to activate them. You have a future. You have hope. You have a Father who believes in you and will never abandon you. He is guiding your steps and giving you wisdom. How cool is that? What's more, He works all things together for your good.

Believing what God says about us can be challenging—especially with years of self-talk that is so contrary. The Bible says to

*Be **constantly** renewed in the spirit of your mind—having a fresh mental and spiritual attitude* (Ephesians. 4:23 AMP).

Changing our mental attitudes means replacing old ways of thinking with new heavenly mindsets—and that process is *constant*. Being renewed in the spirit of your mind requires a lot of patience and consistency. Although tremendous breakthrough can occur in a moment, it usually takes time and persistence. Leaders as well as

Believing your true identity affects everything you do.

newer believers all have issues when it comes to believing truth about themselves. We all have old, junky, self-defeating thoughts that need to go. The best way to deal with them is to identify them, make a determined switch, and replace them with truth.

Many times, a demonic stronghold is established when a false belief has been allowed to remain. We need to confront the spirit realm by commanding the demonic spirit to let go of its hold and leave. You have been given the authority to do this (Luke 10:19, Acts 16:18).

The next few pages are filled with declarations concerning your identity. You may find it hard to sincerely speak some of the declarations because you don't fully believe them. This is a normal part of the transformation process. Don't let this stop you. Look up the verse reference, and talk with God about it. Ask Him to give you revelation about the verse and what it means.

The first step toward living in our true identity is to take a definite posture in truths found in the Bible. We are going to read the verses given below and proclaim them out loud. I like to pace back and forth as I speak, but you can do this sitting or standing or any way you want. Just speak it like you mean it 100 percent. Don't be weak or half-hearted. Whatever you do, do it with all you've got! Live in the power of God's perception of you!

PRAY BEFORE YOU POSTURE

God, breathe life on the proclamations! In Jesus' name, I break off past thought patterns that are contrary to God's truth.

POSTURING: MY NEW IDENTITY

I am a child of the living God. (JOHN 1:12)

I am a new creation with a new identity. (2 COR. 5:21)

I am a friend of Jesus. (JOHN 15:15)

I love being His friend! (JOHN 15:15)

Jesus lives in me. (GAL. 2:20)

I am a citizen of heaven. (PHIL. 3:20)

I have eternal life. (1 JOHN 5:11)

I am accepted by God. (2 COR. 5:21)

I am in right standing with God. (ROM. 5:1)

I have peace with God. (ROM. 5:1)

I am empowered with God's grace! (2 COR. 12:9)

I am loved. (JOHN 3:16)

I am extravagantly loved by God. (JOHN 3:16)

I am forgiven. (1 JOHN 1:9)

My past is forgiven—completely. (COL. 1:14)

Condemnation, get away from me! (ROM. 8:1)

I am not under condemnation! (ROM. 8:1)

I am a new person. (2 COR. 5:17)

I have a fresh start. (2 COR. 5:17)

I belong to God. (1 COR. 6:19-20)

I was planned by God. (Ps. 139:14)

I am special and unique—one of a kind.
(1 COR. 12:12-27)

I am valuable to God. (LUKE 12:24)

I have my own place and function in the body.
(1 COR. 12:27)

I have talents and abilities that are gifts from God. I will not bury them. I will use them. (MATT. 25:14-30)

I stir up the gifts within me! (2 TIM. 1:6)

The Holy Spirit has wonderful gifts, and I eagerly desire them! (1 COR. 14:1)

I have access to God through the Holy Spirit.
(EPH. 2:18)

The Holy Spirit lives in me. (JOHN 14:17)

He reveals truth to me and enables me to do great things for God. (JOHN 14:17, 12)

I am confident that the good work God has begun in me will be completed. (PHIL 1:6)

I will run the race; I will finish the course. (HEB. 12:1)

I am a saint, consecrated and set apart. (EPH. 1:1)

I am forever free from the power of sin. (ROM. 8:1)

I am free from any charge against me. (ROM. 8:31-34)

I am complete in Christ. (COL. 2:10)

I have the mind of Christ. (1 Cor. 2:16)

I am seated in heavenly realms with Christ. (Eph. 2:6)

I am anointed by the Lord to present the gospel. (Isa. 61:1)

I bind up the brokenhearted, proclaim freedom to the captives, and release to the prisoners. (Isa. 61:1)

I am blessed in the heavenly realms with every spiritual blessing. (Eph. 1:3)

I am the righteousness of God in Christ. (2 Cor. 5:21)

I am redeemed. (Col. 1:14)

I am united with the Lord, having become one spirit with Him. (1 Cor. 6:17)

I am established, anointed, and sealed by God. (2 Cor. 1:21-22)

Identity Activations: A New Identity

One. The first activation in every chapter concerns *posturing*. Posturing tears down wrong mindsets and immerses you in your true identity. *Speaking* the verses is the most important and most powerful of the activations. Decide right now that you are going to go for it. Renewing your mind requires decisive action.

Your assignment is this: *Speak* the verses for the next seven days—once in the morning and again right before bed. Also, continue speaking the verses from chapter one at least once every couple days. It's not unusual for me to proclaim quite a few different topics at a time. I carry the verses with me so I can speak them randomly throughout the day. No one can renew your mind but you. It takes diligence, but *you* can do this. Ask God for the grace you need to renew your mind. These posturing verses are designed to build up your *overall* identity in Christ. Subsequent chapters will address more specific aspects of identity.

Two. Activation Two will be the same throughout the study. You are training yourself to identify, confront, and transform wrong mindsets into heavenly mindsets. This can be very, very challenging because a wrong mindset is a lie you have believed as a truth. To build your true identity—the identity God has for you—you must dismantle these lies. Some lies will be very obvious and others will be subtler. By the time you complete the last chapter, you will be better equipped to recognize wrong mindsets and know how to replace them with everything God says is true about you and about Himself.

Posturing in Scripture is a vital part of renewing your mind. Sometimes, when we declare a verse, we have a hard time getting the words out of our mouths. Not fully believing the verse for ourselves indicates that we believe something contrary to the verse. We have believed a *lie* and established a wrong mindset in our thinking. The lie may have entered your life at an early age when harsh or unkind words were spoken to you. Sometimes, when traumatic experiences happen to us, we make an inner decision that is in direct opposition to what God says is true. Sometimes, we arbitrarily decide something is true because we don't know better. Lies are strongholds; they can be demolished. You do not have to live with lies—no matter how long ago they were erected.

Choose a verse you have difficulty believing. Ask the Holy Spirit to reveal the lie you accepted in its place. That lie kept you from believing the verse. Once you have a revelation of the lie, ask God to forgive you for believing this lie. Verbally break the agreement you have had with the lie. Say, "Lord, I am sorry for believing the lie. It has kept me from believing Your Word. In Jesus' name, I break my agreement with that lie." You have begun dismantling a stronghold. Ask God to heal your heart where the lie came in.

THREE. People generally base their identity on performance. Worth is based on how well you measure up to everyone else. Close your eyes and ask yourself, "What makes me see myself as successful?" What is your answer? Think about all the verses in the posturing section. Again, with your eyes closed, ask the Holy Spirit to show you your true identity from God's perspective. Everything He says about you will line up with His Word. Using the posturing verses, write out how God defines your identity.

FOUR. You don't become who God says you are—you *believe* who God says you are. Jesus didn't try to become the Son of God—He *was* the Son of God. Your real identity resides *in* you right now. Your performance does not determine your identity. God loves you the same, even if you do not do anything else for Him. God loves you because that is what He does. He so loved the world that He sent His Son, not because we had done anything to deserve it. So many times when we mess up, we think God is mad or that He will withhold His love from us. Think about this question: Do you feel that God loves you apart from performance?

FIVE. When Jesus asked His disciples, "Who do you say I am?" (Matthew 16:15), He was asking them if they knew His true identity. Simon Peter replied, "You are the Christ, the Son of the living God." Jesus emphasized that Peter did not receive this crucial, high-level revelation from man. The only reason Peter had the revelation of Jesus' identity was because it was revealed to Peter by God the Father—the same One who reveals *your* identity. You find your true identity from God the Father—not from man. Just like Jesus. I feel God is asking us the same question: "Who do you say you are?" So, who do you say you are?

PRAYER: MY IDENTITY IN CHRIST

Father,

Breathe revelation on my true identity. I place my hands on my head and bind myself to my true identity. In Jesus' name, I break off false identities. Lord, breathe on my mind as it is renewed in the truth of Your Word. Wash me—spirit, soul, and body—with the pure water of Your Word. Forgive me for not believing who I am in Christ. I now decree that I am a new creation and all things have become new!

Amen

HEAVENLY WORD

Beloved, I created you as a one of a kind, and I have a one-of-a-kind plan for your life. Do not compare yourself with anyone else. You are unique. There is no one else like you. My desire is for you to see yourself through My eyes. You will find your truest identity in Me, and you will find the *real* you. Every day you are getting the picture more and more—that you are so very special and so radically loved. Yes, I know you have had struggles and have fallen down many times. I use each time to build you back up and transform you. Now, look into My eyes and see My reflection in you. You are My beloved.

PSALMS 139:14; ROMANS 12:2

3

And we, who with unveiled faces all reflect the Lord's glory, are being transformed into his likeness with ever-increasing glory, which comes from the Lord, who is the Spirit.

2 CORINTHIANS 3:18

TRANSFORMED INTO HIS LIKENESS

*Transformed: To undergo a complete change which,
under the power of God, will find expression in
character and conduct.*[ii]

The lowly caterpillar miraculously transforms into a luminous butterfly. Restricted to crawling across sidewalks and through gardens, one day he hides in a cottony cocoon. Then after time he breaks his way out, and—transformed into a glorious winged butterfly—he soars! A most spectacular transformation! A metamorphosis you also experience as *you* transform into the likeness of Christ.

I know it is hard to fathom—that you *can* and *will* experience such a dramatic transformation. But that is exactly what God performs in you—a metamorphic transformation—just like the butterfly. We already studied the Romans 12:2 passage, which tells us to be *transformed* by the renewing of our minds. The word *transformed* is from the Greek word *metamorphoo*. That's right. That's where we get the word *metamorphosis*, which means a change of form or structure. A deeper understanding is vital, so let me share a brief teaching on two more significant passages using this same life-altering word.

The first passage is 2 Corinthians 3:18 and opens this chapter. Look at it again. This verse reveals that as we behold the glory of the Lord, we are being *transformed* into the same image—His image. Like a mirror, we will reflect what we behold. We are being transformed (metamorphoo) into the likeness of Jesus. In other words, we are in a constant state of metamorphosis. Now, let's look at another key verse using this same Greek word. It might surprise you!

Jesus was visibly *transformed* on the Mount of Transfiguration.

> *There he was **transfigured** before them. His face shone like the sun, and his clothes became as white as the light* (Matthew 17:2).

The word *transfigured* used here is also from the Greek word *metamorphoo*. Luke reports this same event, stating the disciples "saw his glory" in Luke 9:32.

When Jesus was transformed on the Mount of Transfiguration, His visage radiated God's glory with such tremendous intensity, it was nearly impossible to look at Him. This is mind blowing! You are being transformed into the likeness of Christ with this same kind of inner and outer intensity! As the power of God's Word works on the deep places of your heart, you exhibit more and more of His love and character. Your countenance will shine with His glory—from the inside out! Even now, as you are reading this, God is orchestrating this supernatural transformation in *you*!

At a Bible study group I was teaching, I asked the participants to think of extraordinary characteristics of people in the Bible that demonstrate how they were being radically transformed into the likeness of Christ. Here's how the conversation unfolded.

"Joshua demonstrated courage and obedience," Chaundra commented. "And he continually asked the Lord for direction."

Heather raised her hand, offering her thoughts: "Paul was humble and transparent, yet he was also strong and decisive."

I added these attributes to a list I'd begun on a large white board and turned to the group. "What else?"

"Perseverance. Joseph persevered through many trials," Landa responded.

"Jael was fearless!" another young woman added. "Can you imagine inviting the enemy into your home and nailing him to the floor with a tent peg through the head?"

"David entered into the presence of God like a child, worshipping in complete freedom," Michelle added.

"I love Deborah," exclaimed Sarah. "She was a warrior and very discerning about how to enter into battle. She prophesied that the enemy would fall at the hands of a woman, and it wasn't even her. It was Jael!"

Kelli had studied the life of Peter. "Peter definitely walked in authority," Kelli added. "People were healed by his shadow."

There are many amazing heroes in the Bible who did incredible exploits and demonstrated wonderful attributes that inspire us all. We can glean from their strength and learn from their mistakes. More importantly, we can acknowledge that the Spirit of God who rested upon them now lives inside us. Jesus heralded John the Baptist as the greatest prophet ever to walk the earth and yet proclaimed that the least in the Kingdom are greater than he (Matthew 11:11). That's you. You get to walk in the fullness of Christ. Jesus said if we believe in Him, we *will* do greater works than even He did (John 14:12).

You may have a hard time believing this to be true because you don't see these *greater works* operating in your life. Your hindrance is that you are viewing yourself from an earthly time perspective. When you see yourself through God's eyes, you step into what I call the *eternal now*. The eternal now is outside of time. This is where God resides, and He sees everything—from beginning to end. God sees you outside of time where your full identity in Him exists. All the facets of your true identity are in full bloom in the eternal now. When you posture in these characteristics, you are tapping into the eternal now/heavenly realm where you are seated. Be encouraged.

God sees you in your future, and you look amazing!

While you are alive on earth, you will continue to grow in Christ-likeness. In fact, the word *Christian* means little Christ or one who is defined by Christ. The reality is that the very representation of Christ Jesus is already in your spiritual DNA. When you received Him as your Lord and Savior, you received a transfusion of His divine nature. This divine transfusion will take its course and work its way out.

Keep in mind, though your identity is already established, you grow in character. Your character reflects your real identity. Maybe you haven't arrived with every detail in place or seen much evidence of this divine nature,

52

but you *can* call forth these godly attributes by faith. Only believe and trust. Something significant occurs when we connect with the reality of the transformation that has already happened inside and call forth its fruit. This is for real. You have godly attributes in you now. They are fully developed in the future you, and you will surely evolve into the future you. So step into the future and call them forth! Decree who you are! Be bold. Be strong. Walk, pace, shout, and feel the power of every proclamation.

PRAY BEFORE YOU POSTURE

God, help me see the truth about what I am speaking.
Breathe life on my proclamations. I break off past thought
patterns that are contrary to Your truth, in Jesus' name.

POSTURING: I AM TRANSFORMING

I am fearless. (2 TIM. 1:7)

I am obedient. (PHIL. 2:13)

I am unbeatable and victorious. (ISA. 43:2-3)

I advance the Kingdom of God. (LUKE 9:60)

I am faithful. (ROM. 12:11)

I am chosen. I am royalty. I am holy. (1 PET. 2:9)

I have destiny. (JER. 29:11)

I am trained and prepared. I know the Word of God.
(EZRA 7:10)

I walk in wisdom. (JAS. 1:5)

I walk in authority and power. (LUKE 10:19)

I confront darkness. (EPH. 6:11)

I know the power of the Name of the Lord.
(PHIL. 2:9-11)

I pull down strongholds. (2 COR. 10:4)

I walk in the miraculous. (MARK 16:20)

I walk in humility, kindness, grace, and mercy.
(1 PET. 3:8)

I walk in the anointing. (MATT. 16:18-19)

I am strong and courageous. (JOS. 1:9)

I speak with boldness. (ACTS 4:29)

I proclaim the Word of the Lord. (1 PET. 3:15)

I am discerning. (HEB. 5:14)

I am a warrior for God. (PS. 144:1)

I am a lover of God. (PS. 84:10)

I am passionate about God. (PRO. 8:17)

I have been crucified with Christ. (GAL. 2:20)

I offer my life as a living sacrifice to God. (ROM. 12:1)

I have favor. (LUKE 2:52)

I am trustworthy. (LEV. 19:11)

I am a good friend. (ECC. 4:10)

I pursue God. (ISA. 40:31)

I am a God chaser. (PS. 42:1)

I am after God's heart. (1 SAM. 13:14)

I enjoy close, intimate communion with God. (PS. 63:1)

I enter into the presence of God like a child.
(Mark 10:15)

I play before the Lord. (Mark 10:15)

I dance; I wave banners; I sit quietly. I worship my
Lord and King in the splendor of His holiness.
(Ps. 96:9)

I am an extravagant worshiper. (Rom. 12:1)

I worship in complete freedom and abandon.
(2 Sam. 6:14)

I am a risk taker. (Judg. 4:21)

I am receptive to the Holy Spirit. (Rom. 8:14)

I do what He says. (Acts 5:29)

I hear God's voice. (Ps. 32:8)

I glorify God. (Rom. 11:36)

I bring peace wherever I go. (Isa. 26:3)

I live in grace. (1 Tim. 1:14)

I am strong and decisive. (Judg. 4:9)

I am a servant. (Eph. 6:7)

I spend time with Jesus. (Luke 10:39)

I am loved by God. (John 3:16)

I love others. (John 13:34)

I am prophetic. (1 Cor. 14:3)

I am active in my spiritual giftings. (1 Cor. 14:1)

I respect the anointing. (1 John 2:20)

I am the righteousness of God in Christ. (2 Cor. 5:21)

I am a peacemaker. (MATT. 5:9)

I have a heart for people. (1 COR. 9:22)

I have compassion. (MATT. 9:36)

I repent. (1 JOHN 1:9)

I forgive. (EPH. 4:32)

I reconcile. (2 COR. 5:18)

I encourage. (HEB. 10:24-25)

I persevere. (HEB. 12:1-2)

I overcome. (LUKE 10:19)

I am free. (2 COR. 3:17)

I am running the race and will finish well. (2 TIM. 4:7)

I am radically and wildly loved by God. (JER. 31:3)

IDENTITY ACTIVATIONS: TRANSFORMING INTO HIS LIKENESS

ONE. Posturing everyday takes discipline. You have to choose to renew your mind and posture your whole being to undergo God's *metamorphoo*. Be strong and persevere. The devil does not want you to posture and know who you are. He will do everything he can to prevent you from believing God's Word. He will make sure you don't feel like doing it—that you're tired or think it's a waste of time. Or that you can wait until the last minute. Or fake it. It takes a warrior to take charge of your thoughts and diligently align them with God. Recognize the warfare.

You know what to do: Proclaim the *I Am Transforming* posturing verses everyday for the next seven days. Carry the book with you and declare them over yourself two to three times a day. If you feel you don't have enough time to do this, say them when you first get up in the morning and before bed as a minimum. Most of us can grab a few minutes then. After the seven days, keep incorporating these verses into your daily life.

As often as the Holy Spirit leads, keep speaking the verses from chapter one and chapter two a few times throughout the week. As you speak these verses, your thought life is reflecting the real you. You are not simply parroting back powerless words. These words are alive and powerful. They are dropping down into your heart and really becoming part of you. That is what a true renewal of your mind is all about. It changes you deep inside. Read through the posturing verses now, and then do the next activation.

Two. Every week, the first two activations are the same, and thus hit the same target. I urge you to jump into these activations full force. Don't think that you've already done it before. Each week contains fresh proclamations, and new lies will need to be dismantled each week. Persevere. Choose one verse you are having a hard time fully believing. Ask the Lord to show you why you are having a hard time with this verse. Most often we heard negative words spoken to us or we spoke them to ourselves, causing us to believe a lie and reject the truth. Lies are strongholds; they can be demolished. You do not have to live with lies. What lie did God reveal to you? Repentance is the door to freedom. Ask God to forgive you for believing the lie. Verbally break the agreement you have had with the lie. Say, "Lord, I am sorry for believing the lie. It kept me from fully believing Your Word. In Jesus' name, I break my agreement with that lie and command any demonic spirit attached to the lie to leave me now! The bondage is broken! Lord, heal the

injured place in my heart where the lie came in. From now on, I believe _____."
Write the verse again in your own words. Ask God to heal the injured place in your heart where the lie came in.

Three. Godly character is developed over time as we experience both trials and victories. With every breath, we recognize more of God's love and grace. What five godly characteristics of King David would you like to see activated more fully in your life? Read a few of the Psalms to refresh your mind about the godly characteristics of King David. Anoint yourself with oil and ask the Holy Spirit to help you develop these qualities.

Four. Read 2 Corinthians 3:18 in a few different translations. Rewrite the verse using your own words.

Five. On post-it notes, write your favorite posturing decrees found in this chapter and place them on your bathroom mirror. You will see them there regularly and have a few extra moments to ponder them!

Transformation Prayer

Dear Lord,
    I am seated in heavenly places, and I see myself from heavenly places! I am transforming into the likeness of Your Son. I am being transfigured—from the inside out. Godly character is being built in me. I yield to the transformational work the Holy Spirit is doing in me. I will see who I am through Your eyes!

Amen

HEAVENLY WORD

Dear One, John the Beloved said, "Now we are children of God, and what we will be has not yet been made known. But we know that when he appears, we shall be like him, for we shall see him as he is." Yes, you are being transformed into My likeness with ever-increasing glory. You are a new creation. The old has gone, the new has come. You will reflect My glory! Do not fear; do not be anxious. It is a done deal!

1 JOHN 3:2; 2 CORINTHIANS 5:17; 2 CORINTHIANS 3:18

4

Look at the birds of the air;
they do not sow or reap or store away in barns, and yet
your heavenly Father feeds them. Are you not much
more valuable than they?

MATTHEW 6:26

TOTALLY ACCEPTED AND HIGHLY VALUED

Valuable: Worth much, precious, highly esteemed.

I sat cross-legged on the floor facing Michelle. We were surrounded by the young women I was mentoring. Looking into her hazel eyes, I said, "Michelle, I stand in the place of the body of Christ. I want you to know that we love you and we need you. We receive the unique gifts God has placed in you. You have a crucial position in the body of Christ, and we are incomplete without you." Tears rolled down her cheeks. As I looked around at the others, I could see that each young woman was also embracing these affirming words for herself. As we took turns honoring Michelle and acknowledging the gifts in her, each young woman allowed the validation of her own personal worth to wash over her own heart. Each member of the body—including *you*—is wanted and needed.

Long before Jesus came into our lives, our self-worth was under siege—mainly from experiences of rejection and abandonment. Even now, I suspect you could describe memories of feeling rejected and left. Rejection means *to discard as useless or unsatisfactory,* and when we experience it, it makes us feel *de*-valued. Our focus today is to embrace our true value as one planned and created by God Himself. Here is a key: God does not abandon you or reject you. God *accepts* you—right now, just the way you are. His arms are always opened wide for you. He is always ready to embrace you when you come to Him. Even if you have been running from Him or ignoring Him. When you return, He is all ready to throw a party to celebrate your return. You are so beloved and special to Him. He *wants* you.

Right now, say "I am valuable. God loves me, and God accepts me." Our ability to grow in the talents God has given us corresponds directly to our own acknowledgment of our individual self-worth. Thus, our confidence grows with the realization that God accepts us. This wondrous truth enables us to also embrace and value others. Our capacity to love others is wholly related to how much we love and accept ourselves. Jesus said the greatest commandments were to love God with all your heart and love people *as you love yourself* (Mark 12:33). How we treat people—ourselves included—is determined by our own self-worth. Here is a key: Our self-worth is solidified in our hearts through believing God loves us and accepts us. Our concept of self-worth is based on our believing our identity. As we know who we are in God's heart, we find true value and self-worth, and only then do we really know how to live.

Most people view their self-worth by worldly standards. For example, a person's worth is commonly based on the kind of home in which he lives, the car he drives, the job he has, the clothes he wears, the friends he has, his level of education, or the quality and quantity of possessions he's accumulated. The devil loves these comparisons. Why? Because you can never accomplish enough or perform well enough; there is always the next guy who has more or who has accomlished more. When we compare ourselves to others, we end up either not feeling good about ourselves or getting puffed up with pride because we think we are so great. True self-worth has nothing to do with performance. It has to do with seeing yourself through God's eyes.

Right now, say "I am going to see myself through God's eyes. My self worth is not based on my performance." Because of God's love, your value rests on two basic truths: God planned for you, and He wants you. You are not an accident. God was thinking about you when He created you. He literally thought you up. He cares about everything that pertains to you—even to the smallest detail. He loves you more than anyone on earth could love you. Because He created you with such profound affection, you are important to Him. God sees you as a treasure.

> *The kingdom of heaven is like treasure hidden in a field. When a man found it, he hid it again and then in his joy went and sold all he had and bought that field. Again, the kingdom of heaven is like a merchant looking for fine pearls. When he found one of great value, he went away and sold everything he had and bought it* (Matthew 13:44-46).

The merchant-man represents God the Father. He places such enormous value on you that He sacrificed everything for you. You are of great worth to Him— *you* are the pearl of great price. You are the apple of His eye. You are the prize He treasures most. Is that hard to believe? When you posture in your true value, you will be strengthened to believe it even more completely.

Right now, say "I am important to God. I am the apple of His eye. I am the treasure He values." You were created with a unique personality, and you have unique gifts. You hold a position in the body of Christ only you can hold. No one is like you, and speaking for the rest of the body of believers on planet earth, we need you. Without you, there is a gap, a hole. Whether or not you realize it, your life is significant. You have been called and chosen to live a meaningful life that has great impact on the people around you. You don't have to be incredibly influential or famous to be significant. It's a level playing field. The most humble, unknown-to-the-world person is significant and of great worth to God.

Before we make purchases, we check out the price tag to see if what we want to buy is *worth* the price. The price we are willing to pay reflects the worth of that purchase. God deemed us more valuable than gold. He equated our worth with the actual blood of His own Son! God established the price tag of your worth.

> *For you know that it was not with perishable things such as silver or gold that you were redeemed...but with **the precious blood of Christ**, a lamb without blemish or defect* (1 Peter 1:18-19).

Think about it: He was willing for the blood of His Son to be poured out so He could have you back. He made a way for you to be reconciled to Him and know Him. How great a cost! And to Him, *you* are worth it! You are worth dying for. Doesn't this take your breath away?

The moment has come for you to grab the bull by the horns and speak the truth of your real worth. As you proclaim these truths as your own, you begin dismantling opposing voices and building on the foundation God has prepared for you. Some of these statements may be new for you to hear yourself speak. Be brave. Embrace your real worth!

Pray Before You Posture

God, help me see the truth about what I am speaking. Breathe life on my proclamations. In Jesus' name, I break off past thought patterns that are contrary to God's truth.

Posturing: Real Self Worth

I am accepted. (John 1:12)

I belong to God. (1 Cor. 6:19-20)

I am secure. (Rom. 8:1-2)

I am forever free from condemnation. (Rom. 8:1-2)

I am significant. (Matt. 5:13-14)

I am the salt and light of the earth. (Matt. 5:13-14)

I am God's temple. (1 Cor. 3:16)

I have been redeemed and forgiven. (Col. 1:14)

I am a member of Christ's body. (1 Cor. 12:27)

I have access to God through the Holy Spirit. (Eph. 2:18)

God created me with purpose. (Phil. 1:6)

Before the foundation of the world, God planned me. (Ps. 139:13, 16)

Before I existed, His eyes saw me. (Ps. 139:13, 16)

God created me and designed me. (Ps. 139:13, 16)

I am no accident. (Ps. 139:13, 16)

God formed me in my mother's womb. (Ps .139:13, 16)

I am a priceless work of art designed by God. (Eph. 2:10)

God sees hidden treasure in me. (Matt. 13:44)

He gave everything so this treasure can be released through my life. (Matt. 13:44)

The gifts that are in *me* complement the gifts in others. (1 Cor. 12:12-18)

God has arranged the parts in the body, every one of them, just as He wants them to be. (1 Cor. 12:12-18)

He carefully planned me and created me. There is no one else like me. (Eph. 2:10)

I am God's treasure—the object of His great love. (John 3:16)

I am worth dying for. (John 3:16)

Because of His love for me, He sacrificed His only Son so I could really know Him and enjoy eternal life with Him. (John 3:16)

I was in God's mind long before He laid the foundations of the earth. (Eph. 1:4)

He planned me and chose me as the focus of His love to be holy and blameless in His sight. (Eph. 1:4)

I am created in God's image. It's in my DNA to reflect His nature. (Gen. 1:27)

God chose me to be alive for such a time as this. He has a plan for my life. (ESTHER 4:14)

In God's book, I am the pearl of great price. (MATT. 13:45-47)

I am blessed in the heavenly realms with every spiritual blessing in Christ. (EPH. 1:3)

I am unique, one of a kind. The gifts God has placed in me are needed. (PS. 139:13-14)

Lord, You have a plan for my life. (JER. 29:11)

Your plans are to prosper me. (JER. 29:11)

You give me hope and a future. (JER. 29:11)

Lord, You know everything about me. (PS. 139:1-5)

You know what I am doing right now. (PS. 139:1-5)

You know my deepest thoughts. (PS. 139:1-5)

You know everything I say even before I say it. (PS. 139:1-5)

You accepted me as Your child. (JOHN 1:12)

All the days ordained for me were written in Your book before one of them came to be. (PS. 139:16)

You chose the day I would begin my life. (PS. 139:16)

Your presence is everywhere. (PS. 139:7-10)

No matter where I go, I can find You there, continually guiding me and holding me close to You. (PS. 139:7-10)

You will never leave me or forsake me. (HEB. 13:5)

A perfect sacrifice was required for You to redeem me from sin and death. (1 PET. 1:7)

There was only one way: the blood of Jesus. (1 PET. 1:7)

I am the object of Your desire. Your love and compassion for me is without end. (LAM. 3:22–23)

How precious are Your thoughts about me, O God. They cannot even be numbered! (PS. 139:17)

I have a unique place within the body of Christ that only I can fill. (1 COR. 12:12)

Just as every part of a body is needed, I am needed! (1 COR. 12:12)

You are mindful of me, and You care for me. You crown me with glory and honor. (PS. 8:4–5)

I am a daughter/son of God right now. I can do nothing to become more a child of God. (1 JOHN 3:2)

My part is to *believe* it. I *believe* it. I *believe* it. I *believe* it. (1 JOHN 3:2)

I was pursued and adopted, handpicked and chosen to be an heir with Jesus. (ROM. 8:15–17)

I am blessed because my eyes see and my ears hear. (MATT. 13:16–17)

I am holy, blameless, anointed, called, perfected, healed, loved, accepted, and much more. Not because of something I did, but because I am in Christ. (GAL. 2:20)

I am not trying to become who God says I am. I *am* who God says I am. (2 COR. 5:17)

I have a new Father and a new identity. (2 COR. 5:17)

My self-worth is not based on performance. (EPH. 1:6)

I have identity and approval from God apart from works. (EPH. 1:6)

God does not forget about me—ever. (PHIL. 1:6)

He began a good work in me, and I am confident that He will be faithful to complete it. (PHIL. 1:6)

I am accepted. (JOHN 1:12)

I am secure. (ROM. 8:1-2)

I am significant. (MATT. 5:13-14)

IDENTITY ACTIVATIONS: YOU ARE GOD'S TREASURE

ONE. Believing the undeniable fact that you are God's treasure is vital for authentic living in the *real* you. You have been posturing in identity. Now it's time to purposefully posture in a specific aspect of identity: your real worth and total acceptance by God. A week of speaking these proclamations will weaken old strongholds of unbelief, so they diminish and fall. Let these truths soak into your spirit and remind you of just how precious you are to God. If you continue speaking the posturing verses from previous chapters, it will certainly make you stronger. Your main focus this week is to solidify your sense of self-worth. Posture in these verses twice a day and watch your thought life transform.

TWO. Over the course of our lives many of us have been told things that were hurtful and devaluing. These destructive words then replayed in our minds over and over again, creating a stronghold. As we discover our true value in God, these old negative voices clash with God's truth. Verbalizing our real worth and value is difficult for many. This chapter is life-changing. Yet, the Scriptures are true: You are *highly valued*. If you had difficulty reading any of the posturing verses from this section, you have probably believed a lie about yourself. Right now, God can free your spirit from that lie and bring healing and value to your heart.

Start with one verse you are having difficulty believing. Ask God to help you see the lie that hindered you from believing the truth. Identify the lie. Quiet your heart. Verbally break the agreement you have had with that lie. Say, "Lord, I am sorry for believing the lie. It has kept me from believing Your Word. In Jesus' name, I break my agreement with that lie and command any demonic spirit attached to the lie to leave me now! I declare the bondage broken! From now on, I believe _____."
Write the verse again in your own words. Ask God to heal your heart where the lie came in. Relax a few minutes. Soak in God's presence. Accept that you have great value, worth, and significance in Him. You are who He says you are—not who the world says you are.

THREE. Look right into your eyes in a mirror several times this week. Point to yourself and say, "You are accepted by God. God created you and planned you! Your worth and your value are based on what God says is true about you—and nothing else! He loves you way beyond what you can even imagine!"

FOUR. When you are feeling down, you are most likely judging yourself with a harsh voice of self-criticism. In Jesus' name, knock it off! God loves you and accepts you. People are what He treasures above all else—and that means *you*. Read Romans 8:38-39. According to verses 38 and 39, what can separate us from the love of God?

FIVE. When you find yourself having negative thoughts toward someone, you are likely judging this person with the same critical voice with which you have judged yourself. Stop yourself and come up with something that you like about him or her. Okay, in some cases it might be hard to find something. Maybe you like his or her hair or skin tone! Find *something*! Ask God to pour more love into your heart for people. You can't conjure up this kind of love—He pours it into you. Ask Him and He will! What are you doing? You are

> *You are significant—God's masterpiece!*

silencing that critical voice, and you will probably also begin to notice that you are not being so hard on yourself as well.

PRAYER: YOU ARE THE PRICELESS TREASURE

Jesus,

Forgive me for harboring negative feelings about myself. You created me, and You did a good job. In Your eyes, I am a priceless treasure. I am sorry for nitpicking myself and complaining about certain aspects of myself. You are awesome, God. I praise You, and I adore you. Thank You for first loving me. Please help me to see myself the way You see me and to have this revelation embedded deeply within my spirit. Help me to truly recognize and understand that You created me in Your image for Your glory.

Amen

HEAVENLY WORD

Beloved, you are the object of My love. You are so precious to Me and so greatly loved by Me that you are worth the life of My Son. I so carefully planned you and wanted you. I see amazing treasures in you. Yes, there are treasures within My treasure! Treasures ready to be unwrapped and come alive! To be enjoyed and multiplied! I made the way for you to find Me. When you chose Me back, I rejoiced! In that moment, you stepped into eternity with Me. And now—a glorious adventure begins!

JOHN 3:16; 1 CORINTHIANS 12

5

*Be kind and compassionate to one another,
forgiving each other, just as in Christ
God forgave you.*

EPHESIANS 4:32

COMPLETELY FORGIVEN

Forgive: An act in which one person releases another from an offense—refusing to enact the penalty due him or her.[iii]

With one giant sweep of my long arm, I swished all of the papers covering the dining room table onto the floor. I was angry, and my fiancé received the brunt of it. He looked at me, looked at his important papers on the carpet, and quietly walked out. He got in the Blazer and drove off. I was horrified. What had I done? I picked up the mess and tried to re-organize it on the table. I had to make this right. I got in my car and drove over to the ranch where we kept our horses. I knew that was where he had gone because it was feeding time. He saw me from afar, and we walked toward each other. As soon as I got to him, I said, "I'm sorry."

Without hesitation, he said, "I forgive you." I was stunned. Such a quick move to forgive was totally out of character for the old Les. But recently, Les had met Jesus, and Les, the new creation, forgave me—just as Jesus had forgiven him.

Each of us has a past. Each of us needs forgiveness. Part of the beauty of reconciling with God is His pervasive forgiveness for everything we have ever done. No matter how big or small—God forgives us for it all. His kindness leads us to repentance (Romans 2:4).

Repentance is telling God you're sorry and then turning your back on the sin. Repentance is a 180-degree turnaround. It's a change of *mind* resulting in a change of *action*. The old ways are left in the dust, and the Holy Spirit takes over to teach Kingdom ways. In God's Kingdom, when we ask for forgiveness, we are forgiven, and likewise, we become forgivers. That's how forgiveness plays out in our lives. Right now, if you have trusted in Christ's payment for your sins, say "I am forgiven. For everything. It's all been washed off, and my slate is made clean." Now you have entered the no-condemnation zone! Say out loud, "No more feeling bad and guilty. Jesus has washed it off. I am *not* under condemnation!"

We can all write a book about how we have been hurt. No one is exempt from having terrible things happen in his life. Our natural inclination is to take revenge... or hurt back...or at least let people know we don't like them—even hate them. In the face of our pain, we take it upon ourselves to enforce justice. We climb onto the judge's seat and hold court, accusing our wrongdoer of his crimes against us. Naturally, we want to let the whole world know about our injustice, so they can rally around our perspective. There's only one problem: Lack of forgiveness binds *us* with chains and keeps *us* from entering into God's Kingdom of intimacy and power. Period. It keeps *us* from living in our true identity. Our identity in Christ includes forgiveness—toward ourselves and toward others. A heart postured in forgiveness truly follows in the footsteps of Jesus.

What happened to you may be horrible. I would even say that God is angry about what happened to you. But the judge's seat is not yours to take (Romans 12:19-21). The judgment seat belongs to God. Only He can see the big picture. Only He is the righteous Judge. It's not your job.

Think about the radical forgiveness you have received for the things *you* have done. Now picture yourself merrily going on your way, and suddenly you remember that someone offended you. Even though you have been forgiven much, you find yourself wanting justice for what they did to you, and you won't let it go. We have all been in this place. When this happens, we may even begin to feel angry toward God for allowing the situation to happen. Although this attitude may make us feel more powerful and in control of our situation, a serious problem arises with this attitude. Jesus said if we do not forgive people their trespasses, our heavenly Father will not forgive us ours (Matthew 6:14-15). Ouch! Jesus also warned us we would be handed over to tormentors (Matthew 18:21-25). Unforgiveness produces inner torment. No peace. No victory. No freedom.

Here is the way the Kingdom works: God heals your heart when you climb down out of the judge's seat and do what He did for you—forgive. Is it easy? Not always. In His strength you can forgive and receive forgiveness. That's right—He forgives you for all the goofball things you've ever done—the good, the bad, and the ugly. All of it. You take the first step by choosing to forgive others and speaking it forth. Jesus takes it from there. Many people won't forgive because to forgive might in some way justify the wrongdoing. No, forgiveness faces the wrongdoing, calls it wrongdoing, and then rises above it, releasing the ongoing damage and pain caused by that wrongdoing. Forgiveness is a choice to trust *God* to be your Defender and Final Judge. This takes deeper trust, and it pleases Him when we let Him handle our case. Forgive others to the point that you pray for them, and freedom will be yours. Your slate will be clean.

Does forgiveness mean the people who have wronged you are getting *off the hook*? Actually, it more accurately means *you* are getting off the hook! You will no longer be in bondage to the person who hurt you, and now it is all God's deal. Your hands are clean of it. And it will feel good.

It is very likely that the first person you need to forgive is yourself. When people don't forgive themselves, self-condemnation and self-loathing creep in. If you ever wake up in the night and cringe when you think about something you did that wasn't right, you are very likely holding it against yourself and condemning yourself. In the same way you forgive and release others, you can forgive and release yourself. You are so special to God—such a treasure to Him—that it grieves heaven when you are so very harsh and unforgiving toward yourself. Say right now, "I forgive myself. No longer will I hold judgments against myself and be so critical of myself. It's over. I *forgive* myself!" Trust God, and He will enable you to love yourself. Nice, huh?

One more thing. We have to forgive the Bride—the church. The Father loves the Bride and is preparing her for His Son. She is not yet perfect. There are many things about her that may have turned you off or hurt you. Perhaps leaders have let you down, abused their authority, or broken your trust, leaving you disillusioned. Maybe you have been betrayed, rejected, dishonored, kicked out, or had your God-given gifts quenched and not received. Even so, you can posture yourself in love and forgiveness toward the church. It feels so good to let it all go and be free from resentment!

You may have anger or resentment toward God. Perhaps situations did not turn out the way you wanted, and you blame God. When we hold onto an offense concerning God, we must set our hearts on what is true about God's nature and character. Two things are irrevocably true: He loves you, and He is good. That is our starting place.

The real you forgives. *The real you* is forgiven. *The real you* is a giver and receiver of forgiveness. A very beautiful, exciting, and integral facet of your true identity is your willingness and God-empowered ability to forgive. You can do this. He will help you. So, let's begin. Get quiet with God and posture your heart toward Him. With a tender heart, begin the wondrous process of forgiveness.

PRAY BEFORE YOU POSTURE

God, help me see the truth about what I am speaking. Breathe life on my proclamations and break off past thought patterns that are contrary to Your truth, in Jesus' name.

POSTURING: FORGIVENESS

Forgive me, Lord, for my sins. (1 JOHN 1:9)

I confess that many times I haven't done what is right but rather have done things against You. I am so sorry. I really am. (1 JOHN 1:9)

I choose to turn completely around and go the other way—in the God direction. (1 JOHN 1:9)

You are so kind and tender toward me. It's Your kindness, Lord, that really leads me to repentance. (ROM. 2:4)

Take me firmly by the hand and lead me into a radical life-change. (ROM. 2:4)

Forgive me for _____. I ask for forgiveness. I am so sorry. (ACTS 2:38)

I repent in the name of Jesus Christ, asking that my sins be forgiven. (ACTS 2:38)

Please baptize me in the Holy Spirit. (ACTS 2:38)

You are faithful and just. (1 JOHN 1:9)

When I confess my sins, You forgive my sins and cleanse me from all unrighteousness. (1 JOHN 1:9)

I am forgiven. (PS. 103:3)

The slate is wiped clean. All my sins are forgiven. (COL. 2:13)

The arrest warrant against me is canceled and nailed to the cross. (COL. 2:14)

You paid the price I should have paid so I could walk free! (COL. 2:13-14)

Without the shedding of blood, there is no forgiveness. (HEB. 9:22)

Because of the blood You shed for me on the cross, I have forgiveness. (HEB. 9:22)

Jesus, because of Your blood poured out on the cross,
I am free. Not just a little free but wildly free!
(EPH. 1:7)

I am redeemed, and I am forgiven in accordance with
the riches of Your grace. (EPH. 1:7)

I am so grateful! Not only do You forgive me, but
also You forget all about what I have done in the
past. You don't hold it against me! (ISA. 43:25)

As far as the east is from the west, so far has God
removed my transgression from me. (Ps. 103:12)

There is no condemnation for those who are in Christ
Jesus. That means me! I am NOT under
condemnation! (ROM. 8:1)

I do not walk according to the flesh but according to
the Spirit. (ROM. 8:1)

I know I need to forgive myself. I choose to stop
replaying scenes over and over from my life where I
know I did wrong. I forgive myself. I forgive myself
for _____. (HEB. 9:14)

Lord God, cleanse my conscience from the guilt I
have wrestled with in my life. (HEB. 9:14)

I am no longer going to accuse and condemn myself
for the things I have done. (1 JOHN 3:20)

Right here, right now, I open my heart and receive
Your forgiveness. (1 JOHN 3:20)

I no longer live in guilt and shame. I come to You,
Lord, with confidence. (1 JOHN 3:21)

Just as God in Christ has forgiven me, I forgive
others readily and freely—this includes my mother,
father, sister, brother, husband, wife, teachers,

neighbors, friends, and also strangers—everyone You bring to mind. (EPH. 4:32)

Forgive me for holding on to an offense. Forgive me for coming into agreement with it. I break my agreement with that offense. (EPH. 4:32)

All of these people I have forgiven, I release to You, Lord. And I pronounce blessing over them. Bless them, Lord. (EPH. 4:32)

I forgive the Bride—the church. I forgive people in the church and leaders in the church for
_____ (MATT. 6:14)

Forgive me for holding on to and coming into agreement with an offense concerning the church. (MATT. 6:14)

I release and bless Your beautiful Bride, the church. (MATT. 6:14)

I no longer hold them captive. I speak love and blessing over leaders and the church. (MATT. 6:14)

As I forgive the beloved Bride, my heavenly Father also forgives me. (MATT. 6:14)

Lord, forgive me my sins, as I also have forgiven those who have sinned against me. (MATT. 6:12)

There have been times that I blamed You, God, for my situation. Forgive me. I am so sorry. Pull out all resentment and bitterness from my heart and set me free. (HEB. 12:15)

You are a good and compassionate God, showering me with unbelievable love and kindness. (ROM. 8:28)

You surely work all things together for my good. (ROM. 8:28)

IDENTITY ACTIVATIONS: SAYING YES TO FORGIVENESS

ONE. Forgiveness is part of your true identity. You are being transformed into His likeness—and God is a Forgiver. The forgiveness posturing verses will lead you into a safe place with God where you can immerse yourself in the forgiveness process. You purposefully posture your heart to forgive. Hold these verses close to your heart and speak them a couple times a day. If you can do this for a week, it will really soften your heart and bring healing to long-time wounds in your heart.

TWO. We are never finished with forgiveness. Many of us put our head in the sand and avoid it. We resist forgiving. In Matthew 18 Jesus was asked how many times we need to forgive:

> *Then Peter came to Jesus and asked, "Lord, how many times shall I forgive my brother when he sins against me? Up to seven times?" Jesus answered, "I tell you, not seven times, but seventy-seven times."* (Matthew 18:21-22).

Forgiving is not always easy for us. Jesus has asked us to do something that is totally contrary to how the world operates—but forgiveness will heal your heart. Offenses come our way with regularity, and our job is to acquire a lifetime posture of forgiveness. The posturing verses you have read aloud require courage. Acknowledging people you need to forgive may reopen old wounds before healing can cover them and restore your soul. Forgiveness liberates *you*. Partnered with God, forgiveness can soak deeper into your heart and become a way of life for you.

Ask the Holy Spirit to show you a person you need to forgive. Get quiet for a moment with God. With the Holy Spirit at your side, speak forgiveness toward that person. Remember, this is a starting place. In the next chapter, we will address getting the hurt place in your heart *fully* healed. Ask God to heal your heart. Relax. Soak in God's presence. Accept heaven's healing balm marinating your heart. Just breathe.

THREE. Because of God's ongoing forgiveness, we are not to suffer from condemnation. For this activation, we are taking to heart the fact that 1 John 1:9 is true: "If we confess our sins, He is faithful and just and will forgive us our sins and purify us from all unrighteousness." There may be situations you have been involved in that you regret— things you've done and things you've said that you regret and need to take to God. Close your eyes and say, "Show me, Lord, where I need Your forgiveness." Quiet your heart and let Him reveal what you need to see. Then, put it all at the foot of the cross and ask Him to forgive you.

> *Feel yourself immersed in God's forgiveness.*

If this is the first time you've asked God to forgive you for things you have done in the past, then it may also be time for you to invite Jesus to be Lord of your life. If you accepted Jesus once, but walked away or haven't been living for Him, invite Him back into your life. Re-commit yourself to Jesus. God is calling you and drawing you back into His arms. Right now, quiet your heart and ask Him to come into your life. Say, "Jesus, come live in my heart. I am so sorry for the things I have done that were wrong and against you. Forgive me of all my sins. You gave Your life for me so I could have a deep, close relationship with God. Thank You for dying on the cross for me. I love You, and I belong to You now, Jesus. I am going to live my life for You! Amen."

FOUR. To prepare your heart for this activation, pray "Because Christ forgave me, I will forgive others. I cannot do this apart from You, Lord. I ask You to help me. Help me to forgive." Ask the Holy Spirit to show you situations in which you were hurt and the people you need to forgive. With His help, create a list. You have already begun the forgiveness process in the second activation. Throughout the week, go through the same process with your list. If you experienced a major trauma, it would be best to get with a mature believer to go through the forgiveness process with you.

Here is a guide for you to follow:

1. Speak forgiveness out loud toward the person you need to forgive. In your own words, choose to forgive him/her.

2. Bring all the wrongs under the blood of Jesus.

3. Ask God to forgive you for holding on to unforgiveness and for holding onto the offense.

4. Release each person to God.

5. Speak a blessing over the lives of those whom you have forgiven.

6. Rest in God's arms of love.

FIVE. It is not unusual for the demonic realm to accuse you of not having truly forgiven a person. Nine times out of ten, this is the enemy trying to torment you. Always ask God first about what is going on. He will tell you if there is more forgiveness that needs to take place with someone. Your first step has been to speak forgiveness toward a person. The Lord will work the whole forgiveness process in you, causing it to drop down into your heart. When accusations come, declare, "Lord, according to Your Word, I have forgiven this person. You helped me with it. I have forgiven _____."

PRAYER: REAL FORGIVENESS

Dear Lord,

As You forgave me, I forgive others. I speak blessings over them. Draw them even closer to You and shower them with blessings. Give them a greater understanding of Your love for them. Give me a greater understanding of Your love for them. Pour healing salve over my heart and heal the places that have been wounded as I continue to proclaim forgiveness. Give me a tender heart toward people. Superimpose more of Your heart over mine. I am so thankful for what You've done for me. Jesus, I love You.

Amen

HEAVENLY WORD

Precious One, I've asked you to do something that is difficult for the world to understand: Forgive others as I have forgiven you. Everything will be laid bare before Me. I know everything. I see everything. I am a just God. Believe Me, I will take care of you. Your job is to forgive and give it to Me. You can do this. I have gone before you and made the way for you. Hand over your pain to Me. I will restore you.

COLOSSIANS 3:13; HEBREWS 4:13; ISAIAH 61:10

6

He heals the brokenhearted and binds up their wounds.

Psalm 147:3

A Healed and Restored Heart

Heal: To repair and restore to its original, perfect condition.

"Ouch, that hurt!" were the first words out of Joanne's mouth. She had hit her head hard on the floor when a large tall woman toppled backwards and landed on her. Worship music filled the conference hall, and nearly everyone's eyes were closed—including Joanne's. Suddenly, clump! She was flat on her back with a big lady sprawled on top of her. It hurt! The words leapt out of Joanne's mouth. In that moment, God spoke to her, "I have been waiting for you to say that." He proceeded to guide her through certain steps for healing deep hurts in her heart. The first step was *admitting the pain*.

Our real identity becomes more fully formed as the emotional wounds in our hearts are healed. All of the pain you have experienced in your life, all of the hurt, all of the betrayal, all of the rejection, abandonment, and emotional abuse—Jesus came to heal. Emotional healing is for you.

Your heart is to be whole. When Jesus announced His ministry in Luke 4, He made a point of saying He was sent to release the oppressed. In other words, His mission on earth included releasing you from all oppression and healing your heart.

Many of us hold on to our hurts like a badge of honor. We try to ignore or bury our pain. When Jesus comes on the scene, He reveals the big wounds we are retaining in our hearts. They must be addressed. It is crucial. To not receive this healing is to deny His compassionate heart being built in us. We will not be able to minister healing to the hearts of other people without experiencing our own inner healing. What's more, when we posture in God's Word, verses go only so far if we have not been healed of major cracks in our hearts. Speaking verses will help, but our personal transformation includes the healing of major wounds. When wounds are not addressed, a life of joy and freedom is hindered. Wounds can put out the fire of love.

Every hurt place in your heart— God heals.

Some wounds require forgiveness. Some wounds require repentance. The healing of some wounds hinges on faith—really believing God for His word. Breaking off the power of words spoken over a person's life can heal wounds. Wounds from physical, emotional, or mental abuse bleed into every new adventure, leaving us feeling hopeless, even helpless, to see that we have a future. All wounds require letting go of the past and not keeping the wound as a badge of honor upon which to hang excuses. Yes, we can build an altar to our wounds and worship them. But don't. If you do, you will soon find your identity distorted by drawing attention to your wound and feeling sorry for yourself. It's okay and normal to admit the pain and feel bad about the whole situation—temporarily.

Just don't stay there. Don't get on a permanent soap box, saying to whoever will listen, "Look what terrible thing happened to me!" Self-pity is a trap that entangles you and keeps you bound if you set up camp there. Keep moving forward through the healing process. You will make it. Jesus came to heal the brokenhearted.

He heals the brokenhearted and binds up their wounds (Psalm 147:3).

Hurt and anger are often linked together. When we suffer loss or betrayal, anger steps right in. Anger tries to cover up the hurt so we don't feel it so deeply. Anger is wicked. It can consume a person, bringing sickness to the body and separation from people. Fear also endeavors to stake a claim in a wound. The fear associated with a wounded heart is usually an abnormal fear that freezes us so we can't move forward in an area of our lives. It is a demonic spirit. Fear keeps us stuck. There is no advancing when we are stuck.

Joanne is a very close friend of mine. For years she has ministered the specific steps the Lord revealed to her for healing wounds of the heart. Though she could write a whole book on it, she has shared with me a very brief version. This is not the only way to heal your heart, but it will give you a good start.

Steps Toward Healing Your Heart

1. Saying, "Ouch, that hurt!" is an admission that somebody wronged you and you actually became wounded. Hurt is still deep inside, even if you try to gloss over it, bury it, and generally ignore it. Admitting the injury is the first step toward healing your heart.

2. The next step is to forgive the person who hurt you. Even if you feel barely ready, begin by simply *speaking* forgiveness toward the person. In the beginning, you might not feel like your heart is in it. Ask God to help you forgive completely—not just with your mouth. The act of forgiving is an unfolding process. Also, ask God to show you if you personally contributed to the situation. If you did have a part, tell God you're sorry for your part. Also, be gentle with yourself and forgive yourself.

3. Usually, a betrayal generates negative emotions such as anger or fear. These initial emotions are normal and part of the whole process of admitting the pain and healing your heart. But if the emotion persists, you may be dealing with a tormenting spirit. As a follower of Jesus, you have authority over the demonic realm. Look at Luke 10:19, and you will see that Jesus gave us authority to overcome demonic spirits. Command the spirit of fear or anger or whatever it is to leave in Jesus' name.

4. Ask God to come and heal your heart, and then believe He is doing just that—healing and restoring your heart. Thank Him for your healing. Remember, Jesus came to heal the brokenhearted. Each of us experiences brokeness at one time or another and needs His healing power. Nothing restores us like the power of God.

By now, the Holy Spirit has likely brought wounds of your heart to the forefront of your mind. That's what He does. God wants us whole and healed. Practice using these healing steps for each wound. With wounds that are seriously deep, get together with a trusted friend and go through the steps. Remember: you don't go around digging into the garbage cans of your past. God Himself unfolds your healing process. Gently, your heavenly Dad brings forth the next place to be healed. We will spend time on this in the Identity Activations.

As you posture in healing the wounds of the heart, God will comfort you, strengthen you, and pour His healing oil over your heart. He is an ever-present help in time of trouble. Speak these posturing truths tenderly as the water of the Word washes over you.

Pray Before You Posture

God, help me see the truth about what I am speaking.
Breathe life on my proclamations and break off past thought
patterns that are contrary to Your truth, in Jesus' name.

Posturing: A Healed and Restored Heart

Every place in my heart that is broken—Jesus heals!
(Isa. 61:1)

Every place in my heart that is crushed—Jesus heals!
(Isa. 61:1)

Shattered thoughts and feelings—Jesus heals!
(Isa. 61:1)

Every place in my heart that is shattered—Jesus heals!
(Isa. 61:1)

Every wrong word spoken over me—Jesus heals!
(Isa. 61:1)

Every rejection, every pain, every hurt—Jesus heals!
(Isa. 61:1)

Every grief, every shame, every fear—Jesus heals!
(Isa. 61:1)

He came to *heal* the brokenhearted. And that means me! (ISA. 61:1)

Jesus is healing my heart! Right here! Right now! (ISA. 61:1)

I may have big breaks; I may have tiny fracture lines. Jesus heals them *all!* (PS. 147:3)

The Lord is so very close to the brokenhearted, and He rescues those who are crushed in spirit. (PS. 34:18)

If I get crushed in my spirit, He rescues me. (PS. 34:18)

Lord, in all of my troubles, You comfort me so I can comfort those in any trouble. (2 COR. 1:4)

You are the God of all comfort and the Father of compassion. (2 COR. 1:3)

I trust in You, Lord, and I do not lean on my own understanding. (PROV. 3:5-6)

In all my ways, I acknowledge You, and You will make my paths straight. (PROV. 3:5-6)

My flesh and my heart may fail, but You, Lord, are the strength of my heart and my portion forever! (PS. 73:26)

You heal the broken places in my heart—You bind up my wounds. (PS. 147:3)

I am standing in Your love that has been poured out into my heart by the Holy Spirit. (ROM. 5:5)

You will wipe away every tear from my eyes. (REV. 21:4)

Love bears all things, believes all things, hopes all things, endures all things. (1 COR. 13:7)

Lord, Your grace is sufficient for me, for Your power is made perfect in my weakness. (2 COR. 12:9)

With all of my weariness and heavy burdens, I come to You—and You refresh me. (MATT. 11:28)

I find peace in You. (JOHN 16:33)

I find rest in You. (MATT. 11:28)

I cast all my cares—all my anxieties, all my worries, all my concerns—upon You because You care for me. (1 PET. 5:7)

Day by day, my inner self is being renewed! (2 COR. 4:16)

Day by day, my heart is being made new! (2 COR. 4:16)

Healing balm of God, pour over my heart right now! (LUKE 4:18)

IDENTITY ACTIVATIONS: HEALING WOUNDS OF THE HEART

ONE. Store these posturing verses close to your heart. They are life, and they are truth. "He sent forth His Word and healed them..." (Psalm 107:20). Spend time speaking them over yourself every day this week, at least once in the morning and once at night. I pray by now you've established a discipline for posturing in God's Word. Continue to say the verses from other chapters as you feel led by the Holy Spirit. You are in a time of renewal. Renewal takes effort and sacrifice. Very likely, you will have to give something up to create the extra time for posturing and renewing your mind. Your belief in your true identity is gaining strength.

TWO. Your heart is in the process of being healed by the Lord right now. And as He heals you, wounds are uncovered. Sometimes the wounds go so deep we have a hard time believing we will ever be fully healed. If you had difficulty reading any of the posturing verses above, there may be a wrong mindset or lie that is telling you you can't be healed. Right now, God can free your spirit from that lie and bring healing and restoration to your heart.

Look at the posturing verses and find one you have difficulty accepting.

Ask the Holy Spirit to show you the lie that hindered you from accepting the truth of the verse. Consider that the lie may be that your experience was too bad, too extreme, and that you cannot be completely healed. Identify the lie you accepted in your heart.

Ask God to forgive you for agreeing with the lie and building a wrong mindset. Verbally break the agreement you have had with the lie. Say, "Lord, I'm sorry for believing a lie. It kept me from trusting You and believing Your Word. In Jesus' name, I break my agreement with that lie and command any demonic spirit attached to the lie to leave me now! I declare this bondage broken! I release the pain in my heart to You. Heal my heart where the lie came in." Relax. Soak in God's presence. Accept heaven's healing balm marinating your heart. Just breathe.

THREE. Jesus came to heal the brokenhearted. (See Isaiah 61:1 and Luke 4:18.) Brokenhearted means crushed, shattered, and bruised. Close your eyes and ask the Holy Spirit to reveal the next place He wants to heal in your heart. Stay quiet and ask Him to soak your heart in His healing oil. Put your hand over your heart and say, "Heart, it's time to be healed." Start with a situation that has a very small wound. Go through the four steps. Remember, when you hit bigger targets, you may want to do this with a trusted friend who is mature in the faith. This four-step healing process is not in-depth counseling. This is a first step for you to do with God. Practice it and incorporate it into your prayer life. If counseling is needed, it would be wise to obtain it.

Four. Read John 14:26 in a few translations. Look at the various words used to describe the Holy Spirit. He is called the Helper, Comforter, and Advocate. Read Acts 9:31. What did the Holy Spirit do for the people? What does comfort and encouragement mean to you?

Once again, with your hand on your heart, close your eyes and say, "Holy Spirit, You are the great Comforter. I receive Your comfort. I receive Your encouragement." Feels good, huh? You are purposefully recognizing who He is and how He helps you. Make this declaration out loud a few more times today and continue throughout the week. Based on these verses, what kind of friend is He to you?

Five. Isaiah 53:3-5 is a prophetic picture of Jesus. From this passage, we learn that He is familiar with our pain and grief and sorrow. Now read Psalm 147:3. God *promises* that He will heal your heart. What wounds has God already healed in your heart?

Prayer: A Healed Heart

Heavenly Father,
Painful things have happened to me. I can't even figure out how some of the pain got there. I ask You to come and heal the broken places in my heart. Heal me from my

past. Heal me from wrong thoughts as I actively pursue getting my thought life renewed. You are so faithful! You said that You came to heal hearts that get bruised, and I need You to heal mine! Lord, bring full restoration to my heart. In Jesus' name,

Amen

HEAVENLY WORD

Precious One, did I not say I came to give you life, and life more abundantly? I carried your sorrows long ago, and I am right now in the process of healing your heart—no matter how superficial or deep the wound may be. I am passionate about seeing your heart whole and healed—and full of joy! My joy is your strength! I will flood your heart with such joy that you can't help but experience supernatural joy and happiness bubbling up inside you. Remember: I restore your soul! The truth makes you free—truly free.

JOHN 10:10; ISAIAH 53:4; LUKE 4:18; NEHEMIAH 8:10; PSALM 23:3;
JOHN 8:32

7

I will greatly rejoice in the Lord, my soul shall be joyful in my God; for He has clothed me with the garments of salvation, He has covered me with the robes of righteousness, as a bridegroom decks himself with ornaments, and a bride adorns herself with her jewels.

ISAIAH 61:10 NKJV

Covered in Righteousness

Righteousness: Just, right standing, right relationship with God.

Have you ever felt like God was mad at you? That you just didn't measure up? That you couldn't do this Christian thing? Very early in my Christian walk, I felt like that. I had a hard time believing God fully accepted me. My former beliefs in karma and reincarnation didn't help. For many years my self worth was based on my performance. The righteousness of God in Christ was foreign to me. Everything changed in a single night.

A local ministry invited me to share my testimony of how God delivered me from a New Age belief system and spiritual deception. After the meeting opened, the worship leader led a song about being covered with robes of righteousness. She said that when God looks at me, He doesn't see what I used to be, but He sees Jesus. Wow! It hit me hard! I was *completely covered*! I was *clothed* in His robes of righteousness because I had accepted what

Jesus had done for me. It was miraculous! Floodgates of understanding opened, and the tears wouldn't stop. I was in *right standing* with God! I was fully loved and accepted!

Righteousness is a major ingredient of your true identity. Righteousness destroys rejection. It destroys feelings of inferiority. If you do something wrong, you are still righteous. If you think wrong thoughts, you are still righteous. Righteousness is not about what you do; it is about who you are. Believing you are righteous is *believing* your identity. When we mess up, a slippery slope leads into an I-need-to-do-works-and-perform trap in order to reinstate right standing with God. Let me give you an idea of how that works.

When we become Christians, we receive salvation as a free gift from God—our sins are forgiven and the slate is wiped clean. Right? Then, as life goes on, we discover we've done wrong. Made some bad decisions, done wrong things, and maybe even said hurtful or deceitful words. Once again, we messed up—just like the old days—and we think we are dirty and unclean. We think, "God won't accept me like this. God won't love me with what I've done. Honestly, He's got to be mad at me! I can't live up to this Christian life!" And we hide from God because the shame is so great. Does any of this sound vaguely familiar?

In a last-ditch effort—if we don't split and run from God!—we scramble, trying to figure out how we can get back in right standing with God. The devil doesn't miss an opportunity like this. He turns the spotlight on our sin. Before we know it, guilt and condemnation sweep in. And we feel horrible and believe God's love for us has waned. We think, "There's only one way to get right with God—I've got to do better, I've got to be better." Evil is crouching at the door, waiting for us to rely on how well we can *perform* and how *perfect* we can be to satisfy God and get out of this disaster. We are embroiled in one big, fat lie: *the lie of having to do works to be acceptable to God.*

Our righteousness—our right standing with God—has nothing to do with our performance. Righteousness was given to us because of our faith in Christ.

> *God made him who had no sin to be sin for us, so that in him we might become the righteousness of God* (2 Corinthians 5:21).

In other words, Jesus died in our place for our sins so that we could be *declared righteous*—completely *justified* before God because we surrendered our lives to Jesus and accepted Him! Let that sink in. You can't get away from it! No matter how you mess up! God's righteousness is huge—H-U-G-E! And it is YOURS! It's all over you like a giant jeweled robe from heaven.

There is no perfect act you can do to reconcile yourself to God.

> *For it is by grace you have been saved, through faith—and this not from yourselves, it is the gift of God—**not by works**, so that no one can boast* (Ephesians 2:8-9).

Righteousness is a GIFT from God. Once you are made righteous, the good things you do come out of relationship with Him. He designed you that way. You have entered into a partnership with God, and now with Him you do awesome, wondrous, magnificent works! It is in your spiritual DNA. These new *good works* are not performance based—they are I-am-the-righteousness-of-Christ based—and they place you in the miracles, signs, and wonders zone!

Speaking the truth about your righteousness in Christ builds a *righteousness consciousness* in you. Because our righteousness is relentlessly assaulted by fiery darts of accusation, proclaiming the truth about righteousness with our mouths and in our minds is vital. I can assure you: Righteousness is a bigger deal than you think. As you speak these verses, your revelation of righteousness will expand. So get going and posture in *The Real You*—building your identity in righteousness!

Pray Before You Posture

God, help me see the truth about what I am speaking. Breathe life on my proclamations and break off past thought patterns that are contrary to Your truth, in Jesus' name.

Posturing: Completely Covered in Righteousness

I am righteous! I am the righteousness of God in Christ. (2 Cor. 5:21)

This means I am in right standing with God. Period! (2 Cor. 5:21)

I am accepted and in right relationship with God. (2 Cor. 5:21)

You became righteousness for me. (1 Cor. 1:30)

I am covered in Your robes of righteousness. (Isa. 61:10)

There are no works that get me in right standing with God. (1 Cor. 1:30)

I have right standing with God because I am covered in the righteousness of Christ. (2 COR. 5:21)

Christ did for me what I could not do for myself. (GAL. 3:13-14)

I am not living under the weight of perfection or performance to receive God's love and acceptance. (GAL. 3:13-14)

I am righteous! Righteousness has nothing to do with living up to rules. (ROM. 3:21-22)

Righteousness has nothing to do with how I perform! (ROM. 3:21-22)

I am no longer afraid, ashamed, and hiding from God. (GEN. 3:10)

I am accepted and dressed in righteousness. (ISA. 61:10)

I am a new creation with a new identity! The old has passed away. (2 COR 5:17)

I am a new creation, and I am in right standing with God. (2 COR 5:17)

Lord, You refresh and restore my life. You lead me in the paths of righteousness. (Ps. 23:3)

In righteousness—rightness, justice, and right standing with You—I will see Your face; I will be satisfied in seeing Your likeness. (Ps. 17:15)

You bless the righteous—that's me! You surround me with favor like a shield. (Ps. 5:12)

Lord, You are righteous in all Your ways and faithful in all You do. (Ps. 145:17)

Jesus, You became the offering for my sin so that I could become the righteousness of God. (2 COR. 5:21)

What a mind blower that I am covered in ALL—I mean ALL!!—the righteousness of God. Wow! (2 COR. 5:21)

I do not have any self-achieved righteousness based on my own obedience to a set of rules, but I possess genuine righteousness, which comes through faith in Christ. (PHIL. 3:9)

I am not turning back. I'm going down the road of righteousness, godliness, faith, love, patience, and gentleness. (1 TIM. 6:11)

I seek first Your Kingdom and Your righteousness. (MATT. 6:33)

Blessed are those who hunger and thirst for righteousness, for they will be filled. (MATT. 5:6)

Fill me, Lord! I hunger and thirst for righteousness. Give me more revelation! (MATT. 5:6)

Your Word trains me in righteousness! (2 TIM. 3:16)

All Scripture is God-breathed and is profitable for teaching, rebuking, correcting, and training in righteousness! Yes! (2 TIM. 3:16)

Having been declared righteous, I have peace with God. (ROM. 5:1)

Fill me with the fruit of righteousness! (PHIL. 1:11)

The fruit of righteousness is peace; its effect will be quietness and confidence forever. (ISA. 32:17)

I approach Your throne of grace with confidence, so that I may receive mercy and find grace to help me in my time of need. (HEB. 4:16)

Your Kingdom is all about righteousness, peace, and joy in the Holy Spirit! (ROM. 14:17)

I have a righteousness from God that comes through faith in Jesus Christ. (ROM. 3:21–22)

The righteous are as bold as a lion! That's me! Roar!!! (PROV. 28:1)

IDENTITY ACTIVATIONS: RIGHTEOUSNESS CONSCIOUSNESS

ONE. People invariably hold on to secret mindsets of performance and perfection. Embracing righteousness shatters the lie of needing to perform to gain acceptance by God. Believing you are righteous destroys lies producing rejection and abandon. You are in right standing with God. Jesus made sure of it.

The price you pay to destroy wrong mindsets and replace them with heavenly mindsets is *time*. Sacrifice time this week to declare the verses from this chapter. Speak them over yourself first thing in the morning, as you're going through your day, and as you're getting ready for bed. Take every opportunity to proclaim these powerful words. Do this every day for at least one week. Remember to include posturing verses from the previous weeks as the Holy Spirit leads you. Even if you read only one additional topic a day, choose the one you need most. It is important to keep going over the previous posturing sections.

Righteousness has nothing to do with performance.

TWO. You are training yourself to recognize wrong mindsets. These lies or wrong mindsets that have crept into your beliefs are strongholds meant to keep you weak and powerless. When you believe a lie, you are not believing what God has established as truth—and this makes you weak. You will be hard pressed to operate in the supernatural ways of God when your mind is deceived. This is exactly why you are uncovering lies in every identity topic in this book. You are learning to identify and demolish lies. The position in your mind the lie had controlled is filled with the living Word of God. This is a life-long practice. I have equipped many to posture, and they are always amazed at how many lies they have unwittingly embraced. You will become more and more adept at discerning lies.

As you declared the posturing verses, did you experience any resistance? First, ask the Holy Spirit to show you one verse in the posturing section with which you felt resistance. What is the verse? When you do not fully believe one of God's truths, it means a wrong mindset is hindering you from believing the truth. A lie creates a wrong mindset. Quiet your heart and ask the Holy Spirit to help you identify the lie. What is the lie He helped you see? Verbally break the agreement you have had with the lie. Say something like, "Lord, I am sorry for believing the lie. It has kept me from believing Your Word. In Jesus' name, I break my agreement with that lie, and I command any demonic spirit attached to the lie to leave me now! I proclaim the stronghold broken! Lord, heal the injured place in my heart where the lie came in. From now on, I believe _____." Write the verse again in your own words.

THREE. Sometimes we think, "After all I've done, God can't accept me!" But the truth is, when you accept His Son, God covers you completely with the righteousness of His Son. Close your eyes and really think about where you have come from and what your life looked like before

Jesus. Now see yourself completely covered in robes of righteousness. What does this mean to you personally?

FOUR. According to Isaiah 61:10, we are covered in robes of righteousness. Let your creativity flow, and draw a picture of what that might look like. What could be on the robe? Jewels? Colors? Feathers? Might music emanate from it? As you draw, tune into what the Holy Spirit is saying to you. To more fully complete the activation, we will do a prophetic act. A prophetic act is to interact with what is true in the spirit realm. Take this robe of righteousness you see with your spiritual eyes and put it on.

FIVE. This last activation can be powerful. You are continually speaking words in your mind over your life. This activation directs you to not only speak over your life out loud, but also to look into your eyes and make personal contact with yourself. Go to the mirror, and looking directly into your eyes, say to yourself: "You are covered in righteousness! The past is gone! You are the righteousness of God in Christ. When God looks at you, He sees the righteousness of His Son!"

PRAYER: REVELATION OF RIGHTEOUSNESS

Dear Lord,

I see it! I come to You with confidence and know You accept me. You love me and accept me. You have covered over anything I've held against myself from my past. I am so grateful! I'm so sorry for the times I've hidden from you out of shame or fear or simply lack of knowledge. From now on, whenever I fall short, I will run to my forgiving Father, knowing that I am the righteousness of God in Christ!

Amen

HEAVENLY WORD

Dear One, apostle Paul tried to live up to the law to gain righteousness—but I revealed grace to him. I want you to really know Me—all about Me. One of My names is Jehovah Tsidkenu, *The Lord Our Righteousness.* That is Who I Am! All righteousness is in Me. I gave you the righteousness of My Son. Because you trust in Him, you stand before Me robed in His garments. I put no condemnation on you. I love you. And when I look at you, I see the righteousness of My Son.

GALATIONS 1:13–15; JEREMIAH 23:6; 2 CORINTHIANS 5:21; ISAIAH 61:10; ROMANS 8:1

8

I have loved you with an everlasting love;
I have drawn you with loving-kindness.

JEREMIAH 31:3 AMP

Extravagantly Loved

Love: An undefeatable benevolence and unconquerable goodwill that always seeks the highest good for the other person, no matter what he does. It is the self-giving love that gives freely without asking anything in return, and does not consider the worth of its object ... the unconditional love God has for us.[iv]

"My girls are the most beautiful girls in the world." My father bragged about his two young daughters to everyone. Though he passed away when I was only four, my mother often reminded me of his love for me—that I was special and that he delighted in me. A child needs to feel loved and know she's wanted. But many parents don't express it, or worse, communicate the opposite. This is where God comes in. He's the ultimate good Father. The real deal. The One who knows everything about you and loves you no matter what.

Every one of us has an innate desire to be loved. We were created that way by a loving Father who wants nothing more than to shower us with His affection. Whether you realize it or not, your very spirit cries out for God's affirmation, to know you are valuable, special, and unique. You have been craving to know that you are accepted, that you are the favorite, that you are loved for who you are, not for what you do, that if you screw things up you will still not be abandoned. A significant part of you will always be unfulfilled until you find this unconditional love.

I am sure you have had experiences when you actually felt loved. It may have been with words, gifts, or an approving expression that said, "I really like you." You may have felt loved by something a person did for you or expressed about you. Perhaps you let someone down and really hurt him, and he forgave you and continued to love you and be your friend. More often than not, love coming from the world can be fickle and fleeting. If you're good, you're loved. If you act a certain way, you're loved. Worldly love always has conditions, basically saying, "If you give me what I want, then I'll love you." Every once in a while you find someone who absolutely radiates love. Just by being around him or her, you feel special, valued, honored—not abused or used. This is the kind of love God has for you, and you can't do anything to deserve it.

> *Your truest identity is saturated with God's love.*

God's love for you is unchanging. He loves you the same whether you have a big Billy Graham Crusade ministry or a hidden, unknown, be-kind-to-your-neighbor ministry. He won't love you any more if you do more good works this month than you did last month. Love is just what He does—it is who He is.

Whoever does not love does not know God, because God is love (1 John 4:8).

God will love you on and on and on and on—through all of your trials, your victories, your boring and quiet times, your failures—everything. There is nowhere you can go to get away from His love. Nothing can separate you from His love. There is nothing you can do to get God to love you more. He absolutely, irrevocably loves you. He made you, didn't He? He formed you from a heart of love. He knows all about you, hears all your inner thoughts you would never dare speak—and He still delights in you! Knowing everything about you, He radically loves you. He desires you just as you are. When you stop trying to hide or pretend and simply want to be able to love God back, He says, "Okay, now we are in a relationship." You find His grace poured out on you, and He enables you to love more fully.

Early in my Christian walk, I frequently arose in the middle of the night to pray. Kneeling at the couch one night, I rambled on and on to God. In the middle of my monologue, I said, "How can I know of Your love for me?"

As I opened my mouth to continue with my discourse, He interrupted me. "How much greater can I show you that I love you," He said, "than to die for you?"

If you feel you have only a small measure of love for God, remember our love for Him originates with Him. He died for us—everyone. There is no greater love than this.

We love Him because He first loved us (1 John 4:19).

The whole point is that if you don't feel very much love for God, you haven't been embracing the love He is expressing toward you. And perhaps, you have not yet postured yourself in love *toward* Him. Stop feeling bad about yourself and step into His stirring love. His love is all around you. Simply say "Yes" to it, yield to it and shoot it back to heaven.

Posture yourself to receive. Choose to receive. Choose to embrace. Right now say, "God, I receive Your love. I say 'Yes!' to Your love. I've put up walls and blocks, and I'm sorry. I command the walls of protection to come down NOW! Walls come down! I open my arms, and I receive Your love!" Dear one, He will help you learn to love. Tenderly...and fully...and with all your heart. As you grow in your own love-walk, you will find more love flooding back to you in response. When you yield yourself to love, your love tank keeps filling up with an endless supply. And then it becomes so much easier to love!

Open your heart, open your arms, and let Him come in. He's pursuing you. He's knocking on your door. When you open it, He comes rushing in. Let go of any preconceived ideas you may have, and acknowledge God's passionate love for you. Get alone and speak quietly to Him. Relax. Let these words of love be as honey on your lips and fire to your soul.

PRAY BEFORE YOU POSTURE

God, breathe life on the proclamations! In Jesus' name, I break off past thought patterns that are contrary to God's truth.

POSTURING: EMBRACING GOD'S LOVE

My Father in heaven loves me with an everlasting love. (JER. 31:3)

His love for me is endless—it never stops! (JER. 31:3)

With loving kindness, my Father draws me closer to Him. (JER. 31:3)

He is always wooing me to draw close to Him. (JER. 31:3)

My Father is always remembering me—always thinking of me. (ISA. 49:15-16)

God has even written my name on the palms of His hands. (ISA. 49:15-16)

My frame was not hidden from Him when I was made. (PS. 139:15)

His eyes saw my unformed body. (PS. 139:16)

Not only did He design me—He made plans for me. (PS. 139:16)

With great love, He formed me in my mother's womb. (PS. 139:13)

I praise You because I am fearfully and wonderfully made! (PS. 139:14)

I am God's child. (ROM. 8:15)

I received the Spirit of sonship. And by the Spirit, I am able to say, "Abba, Father." (ROM. 8:15)

Abba means Dad, and I call Him by this most *intimate* and *personal* name. (ROM. 8:15)

God's love is poured into *my* heart. (ROM. 5:5)

The Holy Spirit provides lavish evidence in my heart of God's love for me. (ROM. 5:5)

I didn't have to clean up my act for God to love me. His love is unconditional. (ROM. 5:8)

God is love. Even when I feel unlovable—God loves me. (1 John 4:8)

My heavenly Father watches me. He is always ready to run toward me when I come to Him. (Luke 15:20)

He wraps His love around me and lavishes me with kisses from heaven. Wow! (Luke 15:20)

Send more kisses, Lord! (Luke 15:20)

No matter where I go, my Father's hand will lead me, and His right hand will hold me. (Ps. 139:10)

God holds a big banner over my life—the banner is called *love*. God loves *me*! (Song 2:4)

My heart is so full of love for Him, and I know He has a wild heart of love for me. (Song 2:4)

God's love and kindness shall not depart from me. (Isa. 54:10)

My heavenly Dad's love is amazing! He is a Giver! (John 3:16)

My Father's love is so sacrificial that He gave His Son so I could be with Him forever. (John 3:16)

I put my faith in His Son, and after this life is over— it's not over! (John 3:16)

I am with my loving Father for all eternity. (John 3:16)

Because my Father's love dwells deeply within me, the posture of my life is to love other people. (1 John 4:11-12)

As I love, His love becomes complete in me. It's perfect love! (1 John 4:11-12)

Lord, I exist because You wanted me! (Ps. 139:13-14)

Your works are marvelous. And that means me! (Ps. 139:13–14)

O Lord, You are my Father. I am the clay, You are the potter. I am the work of your hands! (Isa. 64:8)

I am Your *masterpiece!* Yes, I am! Your *masterpiece!* (Eph. 2:10)

I am created in Christ Jesus to do good works, which You prepared in advance for me to do. (Eph. 2:10)

You have compassion on me. (Ps. 103:13)

You are a Father to the fatherless, a defender of widows, and You take care of me. (Ps. 68:5)

Nothing can separate me from Your love. Nothing! (Rom. 8:39)

You so loved the world that you gave Your only Son, that whoever believes in Him should not perish but have eternal life. (John 3:16)

That's me. I'm living in eternal life right now. (John 3:16)

I am completely and totally saturated in Your *love!* (Rom. 5:5)

Identity Activations: Experiencing God's Love

One. There's a great verse in Proverbs 8:17 that reads, "I love those who love Me, and those who seek Me find Me." We have this one life to learn to love—to fully love and be loved. As for me, I want to have it all. I've had my hurts and setbacks just like you. Be brave. Be bold. Take the posturing verses you just read and step into God's world of *love.* Decree the verses first thing in the morning when you are getting ready for your day and at the end of the day right before you go to bed. These are important times of day. In the morning, you are setting the tone for your whole day. At night, think of it as preparing yourself to fall asleep in God's arms and receive dreams from heaven! If you really want to be dangerous, carry the verses with you and speak them throughout the day. But the minimum for this activation is to proclaim them in the morning and at night. Remember: "For the Word of God is *living* and active" (Hebrews 4:12a). The posturing verses do not come from the world or the wisdom of man. They are directly from God, and God's Word is alive and life changing!

Two. Being loved by God is so fulfilling. His love covers us like a thick blanket. When we know we are loved by Him, we can do anything. But sometimes we have a hard time believing that He loves us. If you had a difficult time speaking any of the verses, you may have believed a lie about God's love.

Look over the posturing section and see where your heart did not fully engage with a verse. Write down the verse. Ask God to show you the lie that prevents you from fully believing the truth about God's love. Then, quiet your heart and ask God to forgive you for believing the lie. Verbally break the agreement you have had with the lie. Say, "Lord, I am sorry for believing the lie. It has kept me from believing Your Word. In Jesus' name, I break my agreement with that lie! I command any demonic spirit attached to the lie to leave me now! I proclaim the bondage broken! From now on, I believe _____." Write the verse again in your own words.

Take a few minutes and ask God to heal the place in your heart that accepted that lie. Ask Him, "Lord, heal the injured place in my heart where the lie came in." If He shows you anything about this wound, write it down and let Him speak life and truth to your heart.

THREE. Activations further *activate* each truth more fully in your life. This activation can be powerful, so don't skip over it. Using the Bible as your guide, write your own personal love letter from God to you. Based on Scriptures, what does God say to you about His love for you?

FOUR. Think of some of the love songs you have heard over the years. Ask the Holy Spirit to help you choose a love song and make it your song with God. Have fun! Change around the words. Here's an example: I love an oldies song that says, "Stay just a little bit longer! Oh, won't you sta-a-ay just a little bit longer!" Only, my heart sings it, "Holy Spirit, stay just a little bit longer...!"

FIVE. Set an atmosphere of love and spend quiet time with God. Light candles, play worshipful music, or do whatever you feel sets the tone. Read Psalm 63:1-8 to God. In the stillness of this time, write your love letter to God.

PRAYER: EVER INCREASING LOVE

Dear Lord,

How can I ever comprehend the love You have for me? Wash over me with waves of Your love. Just like ocean waves sweeping over me—sweep over me with Your love. And with arms open wide, I receive it! I know You love me, and I just want to say: I love You back!

Amen

HEAVENLY WORD

Dear Child of Mine, I love you without reserve—unconditionally. My love for you is without limit and without end. How much greater could I show you that I love you than to send My Son to die for you? Nothing can separate you from My love. I love you without reserve. Unconditionally. There's nothing you can do to get Me to love you more. I love you full throttle right now. Watch for Me throughout your day—I will shower you with kisses from heaven!

JERMIAH 31:3; ROMANS 5:8; 8:39

9

I have given you authority to trample on snakes and scorpions and to overcome all the power of the enemy; nothing will harm you.

LUKE 10:19

POWER AND AUTHORITY
Authority: One invested with power.

The Big Wood River rushed below the wooden deck. We were being married on the patio at Warm Springs Restaurant in the spectacular mountains of Idaho. It was a beautifully perfect June day until my husband-to-be dropped the ring! We watched in horror as it bounced erratically on the deck, threatening to disappear into the raging river below. Miraculously, the ring didn't fall through. I looked into my groom's eyes with relief. Heaven was certainly smiling down on both of us. From that day forth, I inherited a whole new realm of authority. I now held the office of *wife*.

All that my husband and I possessed individually would now be shared as a team. My sphere of influence increased when I said, "I do." His sphere of influence doubled as well. I inherited many blessings from my husband. Now I spoke with the authority of a wife, and all of my husband's authority backed me up. I enjoyed special privileges. I entered heavenly realms and postured for both of us as *one flesh*. We were one—very much like our relationship with Jesus. Because of our betrothal to Christ, we gained an inheritance of invaluable blessings. He is in us, and we are in Him. Upon us, He bestowed His power and authority.

Once betrothed to Jesus, we are instantly seated with Him in heavenly realms.

And God raised us up with Christ and seated us with Him in the heavenly realms in Christ Jesus (Ephesians 2:6).

When Christ was raised from the dead, we—all who would come to believe in Him—were raised up with Him and seated with Him. Being seated with Jesus at the right hand of the Father carries tremendous power and authority for us. Why? Jesus is seated far above all principality and power (everything pertaining to the demonic realm), and all things are under His feet—*all* things! *Under His feet* means He has power and authority over them. Since He is the head and we are His body, we hold this position of authority and power over the demonic realm (Ephesians 1:20-23).

You are the dreaded champion!

It is crucial for you to really grasp this truth. Exercising your authority as a believer in Christ is severely tested. Continually. The devil fights you on your faith. Knowing your authority separates you from living an I-am-barely-getting-by-by-the-skin-of-my-teeth life to a life of I-know-who-I am, and I know I-am-equipped-to-operate in the power and authority of Christ. We are not told to ask God to do something about the devil—we all have authority over the devil. Power and authority are given to *you!*

When we make proclamations, our words carry *His* power and authority. It is the authority of Christ delegated to His Bride—us! We are *partners* with Him. The ministry that rested upon Jesus was passed on to us (Isaiah 61:1-3). We proclaim freedom for the captives! Through Christ in us, we bind up the brokenhearted. Through us, people are set free from demonic oppression. Through us, people are healed, restored, and set free.

To confirm the fact that power and authority have been delegated to us, we need to see a few additional key Scriptures. First, *all* authority has been given to Jesus.

> *Then Jesus came to them and said, "All authority in heaven and on earth has been given to Me"* (Matthew 28:18).

Next, Jesus delegated His authority to us. In Luke 10:19, Jesus said,

> *I have given you authority to trample on snakes and scorpions and to overcome all the power of the enemy; nothing will harm you.*

The word *authority* is interchangeable with *power.* Jesus has all authority (power) in heaven and on earth, and He has delegated His authority (power) to His Bride. We have delegated authority. Delegated authority is authority obtained from another who has authority.

Furthermore, in Matthew 6:10, Jesus directed us to proclaim, "Your kingdom come, Your will be done on earth as it is in heaven." We proclaim that which is true in heaven to be manifested on earth. We proclaim God's will on earth. How do we know His will? We read His Book and study how the apostles had authority and how Jesus demonstrated authority. For one thing, Jesus came to heal *all* who were under the power of the devil

(Acts 10:38). Let's start with you. You have authority over your thoughts and emotions. You have been exercising authority over wrong mindsets by proclaiming verses to renew your mind and bring you into agreement with the Father.

Another important aspect of authority is found in the power of the name of Jesus. Jesus not only gave us the authority to do what He did when He walked the earth, but also He told us to do it in His name. Why invoke the name of Jesus? The name of Jesus is above all names. There is power in His name. At the name of Jesus, every knee will bow in heaven and on earth (Philippians 2:9-11). In John 14, Jesus directs us to ask in His name.

> *I tell you the truth, anyone who has faith in Me will do even greater things than these, because I am going to the Father. And I will do whatever you ask in **My name**, so that the Son may bring glory to the Father. You may ask Me for anything in **My name**, and I will do it* (John 14:12-14).

We are the ones who must choose to maintain an aggressive posture so that God's will and purposes may be established on earth. Consider King David. In Psalm 18:37, he states, "I pursued my enemies and overtook them, and I did not turn back until they were consumed." He did not allow any ground to be held by his enemy. When the Lord led him into war, David completely destroyed his enemies. Like David, you are going after your adversary with purpose by praying and proclaiming. Even so, your situation may not change as quickly as you would like. Do not get discouraged. You are on track. Some victories are instantaneous, but others require a full on war that must be won, one battle at a time.

With Christ's authority we are able to *defy* and *overcome* all the power of the enemy.

I have given you authority to trample on snakes and scorpions and to overcome all the power of the enemy; nothing will harm you (Luke 10:19).

Jesus proclaimed the very gates of hell shall not prevail when we rise up in the revelation of whom He has declared us to be (Matthew 16:18). The same anointing that was upon Jesus, empowering Him to destroy the works of the devil, is upon *you*. The same Holy Spirit who was upon Jesus, enabling Him to preach the gospel with a demonstration of power, is also with *you*. When Jesus was given all authority in heaven and on earth, He turned around and delegated it to *you*. You have the same amount of authority as the Apostle Paul or Billy Graham or your pastor. Don't run around trying to get someone else to fight for you. *You* fight. *You* exercise your authority. Together, as His body, not only have we been supplied with everything we need to be free from oppression, but we also have the power and authority to set others free.

When speaking these verses, confront any passivity by taking a defiant stance. Stand strong! Decree strong! War strong! As these truths establish a new mindset, they will then drop down into your being where they will resonate with the reality of the authority Jesus gave you. Authority does not increase in a believer. It is a done deal. Authority is in you right now. We all have the same amount of authority. The difference is in what you *believe* about your authority and what you *do* with your authority. Let us begin to posture in authority!

Pray Before You Posture

God, help me see the truth about what I am speaking. Breathe life on my proclamations and break off past thought patterns that are contrary to Your truth, in Jesus' name.

POSTURING: POWER AND AUTHORITY

All authority in heaven and on earth has been given to Jesus. (MATT. 28:18)

Jesus gave me *power* and *authority*—His authority—to do His work on earth. (LUKE 10:19)

I have authority. (LUKE 10:19)

I have authority to overcome all the power of the enemy! (LUKE 10:19)

Snakes and scorpions are symbols of demonic power. (LUKE 10:19)

I trample on snakes and scorpions. (LUKE 10:19)

Nothing will harm me! (LUKE 10:19)

I am seated in heavenly places with Christ Jesus, where all things are under His feet. (EPH. 2:6; 1:22)

I understand the realm of the spirit, and I operate in the realm of the spirit. (EPH. 2:6)

I am fully aware that spirits submit to me. (LUKE 10:20)

But I do not rejoice that spirits submit to me. I rejoice that my name is written in the Lamb's Book of Life. (LUKE 10:20)

I *know* and *believe* I have delegated authority, and I use it. (LUKE 10:19)

I do not have the spirit of fear. (2 TIM. 1:7)

When fear comes, it is not from God. (2 TIM. 1:7)

I trample fear! (LUKE 10:19)

I trample doubt and unbelief! (LUKE 10:19)

I trample demonic oppression! (LUKE 10:19)

I have the spirit of power. (2 TIM. 1:7)

I have the spirit of love. (2 TIM. 1:7)

I have the spirit of a sound mind. (2 TIM. 1:7)

Miraculous signs follow me. (MARK 16:17)

I cast out demons. (MARK 16:17)

I speak in new tongues. (MARK 16:17)

I put my hands on the sick, and they get well.
(MARK 16:18)

No weapon formed against me shall prosper.
(ISA. 54:17)

Every tongue that rises against me in judgment, I
condemn. (ISA. 54:17)

The God of peace crushes Satan under my feet!
(ROM. 16:20)

The Lord has made me into a threshing sledge over
demonic powers, new and sharp, with many teeth.
(ISA. 42:15)

I thresh the mountains standing in my way, and I
crush them. I reduce the hills to chaff. (ISA. 42:15)

Greater is He who is in me than he who is in the world.
(1 JOHN 4:4)

I submit to God. (JAS. 4:7)

I resist the devil. And he must flee! (JAS. 4:7)

I do not give place to the devil. (EPH. 4:27)

I take possession of what is mine. (EPH. 4:27)

Whatever I bind on earth will be bound in heaven; whatever I loose on earth will be loosed in heaven. (MATT. 18:18)

At the *name* of Jesus every knee shall bow in heaven and on earth. (PHIL 2: 10)

The *name* of Jesus is above every other name. (PHIL 2: 9)

I pray in the *name* of Jesus! (JOHN 14:14)

I pray prayers of faith. Whatever I ask in His name shall be done. (JOHN 14:14)

I pray according to Your Word. (JOHN 15:7)

The Lord enables me to speak His Word with great boldness! (ACTS 4:29)

The exceeding greatness of God's power is at work in me! Right here! Right now! (EPH. 1:19-20)

The ministry of Jesus is upon me! (JOHN 14:12)

The authority of Jesus is upon me! (EPH. 1:20-23)

I heal the broken hearted. (LUKE 4:18)

I proclaim freedom to the captives. (LUKE 4:18)

I bring deliverance to those who are oppressed. (LUKE 4:18)

I build myself up in my most holy faith by praying in the Holy Spirit. Hoo-aah! (JUDE 20)

I am not passive. I imitate those who through faith and patience inherit the promises of God. (HEB. 6:12)

I fix my eyes not on what is seen, but on what is unseen. What is seen is temporary; what is unseen is eternal. (2 COR. 4:18)

In faith, I can say to an insurmountable problem, "Be removed and be cast into the sea." (MARK 11:23-24)

I do not doubt in my heart. (MARK 11:23-24)

Faith is the key. (MARK 11:23-24)

Whatever things I ask when I pray, I believe that I receive them, and I will have them! (MARK 11:23-24)

Jesus disarmed the principalities and powers and made a public spectacle of them, triumphing over them by the cross! (COL. 2:15)

Through the church—that means through me!—the manifold wisdom of God is made known to the rulers and authorities in heavenly realms. (EPH. 3:10)

I say to hurt and broken people, "Silver or gold I do not have, but what I do have I give you. In the name of Jesus, rise up and walk!" (ACTS 3:6)

I operate in power and authority! (LUKE 10:19)

IDENTITY ACTIVATIONS: YOUR AUTHORITY AS A BELIEVER

ONE. Every topic in *The Real You* addresses a promise and presents a teaching on obtaining that promise. Each time you take a stance (posture) in the truth of God's Word, you weaken a stronghold of passivity and build confidence in your authority. Passivity wants us to ignore the spiritual war, to lay aside our swords and forget about our authority. Passivity is grounded in unbelief. We need to learn how to fight battles and not run from our calling and authority. Feel the stirring deep down inside rising up in you. Listen to the still, small voice reminding you of who you are in Christ, encouraging you to yield your life to Him. Just as you have received Jesus, so walk in Him. Envision the greatness God has placed in you, and step into the center of the ring. He has equipped you to stand against the schemes of the enemy and take hold of all your inheritance in Christ Jesus. Come on! If you want it, you are well able to obtain it! Posture in the authority verses twice a day—morning and night. Establish a mindset of God's authority working through you.

Two. Choose one verse you are having difficulty believing. Ask God to help you see the lie that hindered you from believing the truth. Remember, a lie is a wrong mindset you have held onto. Identify the lie. Quiet your heart. Verbally break the agreement you have had with the lie. Say, "Lord, I am sorry for believing the lie. It has kept me from believing Your Word. In Jesus' name, I break my agreement with that lie and command any demonic spirit attached to the lie to leave me now! I proclaim that the bondage is broken! From now on, I believe _____." Write the verse again in your own words.

Ask God to heal your heart where the lie came in. Relax. Soak in God's presence. Accept the truth that His authority and power lives in you right now. See it! Feel it!

THREE. Take a look at the posturing verses. Choose a favorite verse and write it out. With this activation, you will take the verse with you in prayer and study for deeper understanding. With each verse, there are unending layers of revelation. Ask God about the verse. Ask Him to open the eyes of your heart for more understanding. Ask Him for the Spirit of wisdom and revelation concerning the verse.

Look up the verse in several translations and write it out. Also look up key words in the verse. Write the definitions. Now paraphrase the verse in everyday language. Write your paraphrased verse in first person.

Did you receive additional revelation when you continued to pray and study the verse?

FOUR. Read the verses in chapter one. Now, with this fresh posture of authority approach these verses. Taking authority over wrong mindsets with newly gained knowledge of your authority, will alter how you interact with these verses. How is speaking the verses about your thought life different for you now?

FIVE. You will gain greater understanding when you investigate two Greek words for power and authority: *Dunamis* (Strong's 1411) and *exousia* (Strong's 1849). Look these words up in reference books and online. How are these words used? What insights does this research give you about power and authority?

PRAYER: YOUR AUTHORITY IN CHRIST

Father,

Jesus was given all authority, and He has delegated authority to me. What an amazing gift! I do not shy away from what You have given me. I live my life in power and authority. Forgive me for times I have been passive. I break a passive spirit off me right now, in Jesus' name. My faith is not connected to my feelings; my faith is aligned with my authority. Your power and authority reside in me. I am thankful for it! I am fully aware of it! I operate in power and authority!

Amen

Heavenly Word

Beloved, All authority in heaven and on earth has been given to My Son. You are yoked with My Son, and His authority works through you. On earth, your hands are His hands. When you speak, ask Him to fill your mouth. He will do it. Signs will accompany you. You will drive out demons, speak in new tongues, lay hands on the sick, and they will recover. Go and make disciples of all nations, baptizing them in the name of the Father and of the Son and of the Holy Spirit and teaching them to obey everything Jesus commanded you. And surely I will be with you always, to the very end of the age. I love you, beloved. Victory is already yours.

Matthew 28:18-20; Luke 10:19; Mark 16:15-20

10

Who is it that overcomes the world?
Only he who believes that Jesus is the Son of God.

I JOHN 5:5

CREATED TO OVERCOME

Overcome: To conquer, prevail, come through victoriously.

God wouldn't call you to be an overcomer if there weren't anything to overcome. In this life you will run into obstacles of all kinds. If you discern each situation from a heavenly realm vantage point, your insurmountable hurdles will look vastly different. Under the shadow of the Almighty, they are put in perspective. They have no power to defeat you. Set your mind to see things from God's perspective. Your heavenly Dad says victory is already yours. Fight backwards. Don't fight toward victory—fight *from* victory. You are fully equipped with everything you need to overcome. You are *created* to be an overcomer!

Perhaps you don't see yourself as an overcomer, and you have a list of reasons why you do not qualify. Well, whether you feel like it or not, God not only says you are called to be an overcomer, but He also says you already *are* an overcomer. Why? For the sole reason that you *believe* Jesus is the Son of God and that He died in your place to reconcile you into a relationship with God. First John 5:5 states, "Who is it that overcomes the world? Only he who believes that Jesus is the Son of God." Our part is to *choose* the posture of an overcomer and *believe* God. Be determined to see yourself through God's eyes. God proclaims you an overcomer even *before* you overcome anything. Gideon is a great example.

When Gideon was hiding and cowering in the winepress, God called out to him, "Gideon, O mighty man of valor" (Judges 6:12, ESV). Gideon, a mighty man of valor? Besides acting like a coward, Gideon had a list of reasons why he was not a brave or mighty man. He pulled those rehearsed credentials out when the angel of the Lord addressed him. He was from the weakest clan. And he was also the biggest wimp of his clan! "And he said to Him, 'Please, Lord, how can I save Israel? Behold, my clan is the weakest in Manasseh, and I am the least in my father's house'" (Judges 6:12, ESV). God, however, saw Gideon in his future. He saw him as a mighty warrior. So it is with you. Even though you may not see yourself as a champion, God sees you in your future—and not in linear time. In an earlier chapter, we noted that God sees you in the eternal now. He sees you in your future. I love Kim Clement's song, "You're somewhere in the future, and you look much better than you look right now!" The future you is in you right now. God has decreed it. He sees the whole you. The DNA of a champion has already been downloaded into you.

When I have a huge mountain in front of me, I am strengthened by Joshua's story. God encouraged Joshua before he led the Israelites into the Promised Land:

> *Be strong and of good courage; do not be afraid, nor be dismayed, for the Lord your God is with you wherever you go* (Joshua 1:9 NKJV).

Through this word to Joshua, God is also speaking to us to be strong and courageous. Our strength and courage are centered in the abiding presence of Jesus. He goes before us as a mighty breaker—breaking open the way for us to overcome opposition. His glory is our rear guard (Isaiah 58:8). Every day you have the opportunity to apprehend another promise and conquer another portion of your Promised Land. Every victory you win becomes more territory, more promises, to possess. Each time you overcome opposition, your opposition loses its power and no longer has jurisdiction over you. That which you overcome—you own!

What we declare with our mouths makes all the difference.

*And they overcame him [the devil] by the blood of the Lamb and by the **word of their testimony**, and they did not love their lives so much as to shrink from death (Revelation 12:11).*

The words you speak matter! You overcome by the *word* of your testimony. Now you know God sees you as an overcomer, and He calls you an overcomer. As you posture, you will simply say what God has ordained. Today we posture as overcomers!

PRAY BEFORE YOU POSTURE

God, help me see the truth about what I am speaking.
Breathe life on my proclamations and break off past thought
patterns that are contrary to Your truth, in Jesus' name.

POSTURING: POSITIONED AS AN OVERCOMER

I am an overcomer because I believe Jesus is the Son of God! (1 JOHN 5:5)

By the blood of the Lamb and by the word of my testimony, I overcome demonic assignments. (REV. 12:11)

Lord, Your blood made the way for me to be an overcomer! (REV. 12:11)

I overcome by the confession of my mouth. That means I boldly declare who God is, who He says I am, and what He has done for me. (ROM. 10:9)

I boldly declare God is faithful to me! (LAM. 3:23)

I boldly declare God loves me outrageously! (JER. 31:3)

I boldly declare that with every trial, every hard place, every ache in my heart, He is with me, carrying me through it. (2 COR. 9:8)

I boldly declare multitudes will come into the Kingdom of God through my life. (MATT. 4:19)

I boldly declare I am flooded with compassion. (COL. 3:12)

I boldly declare supernatural love flows through me. (ROM. 5:5)

I boldly declare I am relentless in my pursuit of God. (PS. 105:4)

I boldly declare I often withdraw to lonely places to pray. (PS. 105:4)

I boldly declare I am a warrior. (LUKE 10:19)

I boldly declare I overcome the demonic realm! Through Christ, I am fearless! Death does not reign over me. (HEB. 2:14-15)

Through Christ, I push back demonic powers and trample demonic forces. (Ps. 44:5)

I pursue my enemies and overtake them; I do not turn back until strongholds in opposition to God are demolished. (Ps. 18:37)

My faith is the reason for my victory! (1 JOHN 5:4)

I will not lose hope. God amply supplies me with all the faith I need for victory! (ROM. 15:13)

Victory is mine already! I fight *from* the place of victory! (ROM. 15:13)

The same spirit of faith in which Christ Jesus walked and that raised Him from the dead is living in me! (2 COR. 4:11-14)

I throw off everything that hinders and the sin that so easily entangles. (HEB. 12:1)

I run with perseverance the race marked out for me. (HEB. 12:1)

I fix my eyes on Jesus, the author and finisher of my faith. (HEB. 12:2)

He ran this race, and I am training under Him! (HEB. 12:2)

I think of Jesus who endured such hostility, so that in the face of all my trials I will not grow weary and lose heart. (HEB. 12:3)

I am made holy by the Truth. (JOHN 17:17)

I am born of God, and I am victorious over the ways of the world. (1 JOHN 5:4)

I can do ALL things through Christ who strengthens me. (PHIL. 4:13)

My mind is not focused on the desires of the flesh; my mind is set on what the Spirit desires. (ROM. 8:5)

When I put my hand to the plow, I do not look back. (LUKE 9:62)

I am not conformed to the world, but I am transformed by the renewing of my mind. (ROM. 12:2)

I am an overcomer both physically and spiritually. God forgives all my sins and heals all my diseases. (Ps. 103:3)

I am not overcome by evil. I overcome evil with good. (ROM. 12:21)

The Holy Spirit intercedes for me, praying God's will for me with groans that words cannot express. I yield to His will. (ROM. 8:26-27)

I have been given authority to trample on snakes and scorpions and to overcome all the power of the enemy; nothing will harm me! (LUKE 10:19)

Through trouble or hardship or persecution or famine, I am more than a conqueror through Christ who loves me! (ROM. 8:37)

I am an overcomer in my thought life! (2 COR. 10:5)

I am victoriously living in my true identity! (2 COR. 5:17)

Jesus will write on me the name of God, the name of the city of God, and His new name. I am a fully claimed possession of God! (REV. 3:12)

I am an overcomer, and I will be given the right to eat from the tree of life. (REV. 2:7)

I am an overcomer, and I will receive hidden manna from the Lord; I will be given a white stone with a new name written on it. (REV. 2:17)

I am an overcomer, and I will be given authority over nations. (REV. 2:26)

I am an overcomer, and I will be given the crown of life. (REV. 2:10)

I am an overcomer, and my name will never be erased from the Book of Life. (REV. 3:5)

I am an overcomer, and I will be a pillar in the temple of my God. (REV. 3:12)

I am an overcomer, and I will be given the right to sit with Jesus on His throne. (REV. 3:21)

I am an overcomer. I have an eternal inheritance. I will receive all that He has. I will forever be a child of God. (REV. 21:7)

I am an overcomer! I am an overcomer! I am an overcomer! (1 JOHN 5:5)

IDENTITY ACTIVATIONS: ACTIVATING THE OVERCOMER IN YOU

ONE. Declaring yourself an overcomer is powerful. The devil does not want you to think like this. He comes to steal your true identity and destroy it. You have to fight for it. You have to be like Jesus and say, "It is written!" Recognize that there is a war going on! You have to fight to change your mindsets to posture yourself as an overcomer. Trials and difficulties will come. You must *believe* this vital truth about your identity! You must conquer this land! I speak to you as a mother in the faith. Do not wonder if you are going to make it—if you can overcome. *Know* and *believe* you have been endued with power from God to overcome! Because it can take

You are designed to overcome every obstacle.

time to rewire your mindsets and believe you are an overcomer, this activation is imperative. Speak these verses twice a day. This day you fight!

Two. Trials are difficult. At times, we wonder how we will get through them. We cannot see an end in sight. This is exactly why it is vital that we see ourselves as overcomers. Choose a verse you have had difficulty reading in the posturing section. You probably have believed a lie about yourself and have doubted God's Word. Right now, you can be free. First, ask God to help you see the lie that hindered you from believing truth. Identify the lie. Quiet your heart. Ask God to forgive you for believing the lie. Verbally break the agreement you have had with the lie. Say, "Lord, I am sorry for believing the lie. It has kept me from believing Your Word. In Jesus' name, I break my agreement with that lie and command any demonic spirit attached to the lie to leave me now! I declare the bondage is broken! Lord, heal the injured place in my heart where the lie came in. From now on, I believe _____." Write the verse again in your own words. Relax. Soak in God's presence, accepting the absolute truth that you are an overcomer. You will make it. You will finish the race and finish well. You are an overcomer.

Three. The next activation is a concept I gleaned from worship leader Jake Hamilton. Meditate on the opening verse for this chapter, 1 John 5:5. If you take your time with this, you will begin to imbed the revelation of this verse in your heart. It can take time for a verse to move from your head down to your heart. So take your time and enjoy the process. God loves spending time with you. And He really wants to take you way below the surface of the words on a page.

Begin by writing the verse at the top of a blank page. Slowly speak it out loud and ponder every word. Think of yourself as doing this with God.

Next, write it out creatively. Draw pictures, doodle, and interact with it. Try speaking the verse over and over, emphasizing different words.

Explore singing it. Spend time singing it, whether you think you can sing or not. God likes you, and He likes you singing His Word. Get creative. Even dance!

Finally, pray it. Really explore the verse in prayer.

FOUR. What obstacle are you facing? Ask the Holy Spirit to help you complete the following sentence: In my life right now, in order for me to move forward, I must overcome

_____.

Ask the Holy Spirit to show you your next step in overcoming. Plan and take the first step in overcoming this specific obstacle. You might ask a close friend (who is a positive influence) to help hold you accountable in this forward motion.

FIVE. God is calling you just like He called Gideon. You may be hiding in the middle of your own winepress. But God is calling you a mighty man or woman of valor. Ask the Holy Spirit to show you what you look like as an overcomer. Take the image He impresses on you and draw it. Draw your own wildly creative picture of you as an overcomer. This is a prophetic act. You are activating the overcomer in you with a visual.

PRAYER: BEING AN OVERCOMER

God,

No matter what I face in life—I am an overcomer! I *posture* myself as an overcomer. I *see* myself as an overcomer. Nothing is going to take me out prematurely. I posture myself with a persevering spirit. I will not give up or back down. Through Your grace and strength, I prevail! Lord, do through me immeasurably more than all I can ask or imagine! In Jesus' mighty name.

Amen

HEAVENLY WORD

Beloved, I am the Alpha and the Omega, the Beginning and the End. I know all things; I see all things. I am your Great Provider, and I have given you all you need to be like My Son. You are an overcomer. He who overcomes will inherit much from Me. Come up here and look down from where you are seated in My heavenly realms. The view is different from up here. Catch My vision. Live from your true identity.

REVELATION 21:6–7; EPHESIANS 2:6

BONUS ARTICLE

31 WAYS GOD SEES YOU RIGHT NOW

*M*ost people see themselves through the eyes of the world. Wouldn't you love to know how God sees you? You can. By looking at Scriptures from the Old and New Testaments, you can learn what God really thinks about you. You can discover how He feels about you, what He says about your future, and about all of the qualities He sees in you. You may not see them, but He does. Embrace how God sees you; embrace His thoughts toward you. God's view of you is unchanging. He loves you beyond anything you can imagine. He wants you to feel good about yourself!

As you read this list, speak the words quietly to yourself. Even though you may not see these qualities in your life right now, they are resident within you. Your soul is coming into agreement with heaven!

Right now, God sees you as:

1. Spotless and beautiful.

2. Speaking with a voice that shakes the heavens.

3. Filled and overflowing with liquid love.

4. Moving in great wisdom, able to discern between good and evil.

5. Outrageously loved.

6. Totally accepted.

7. Completely forgiven.

8. Righteous.

9. An heir—freely coming into His presence.

10. A lover and a warrior.

11. An overcomer.

12. Healed and whole.

13. Ruling and reigning with Him.

14. Seated in heavenly realms.

15. A laughing Bride—laughing at fear, afraid of nothing!

16. A compassionate Bride.

17. Pure—your face shining with His glory.

18. Having piercing eyes—moving in authority.

19. A supernatural being—doing supernatural acts in the natural world.

20. Dreaming with Him.

21. Swaying, bending, yielding, being moved by the wind of the Spirit.

22. Possessing quiet confidence.

23. Bold as a lion.

24. A deeply intimate friend.

25. Trusting in His Word—not in circumstances.

26. Faithful lover.

27. A worshipper.

28. Dancing through the universe with Him.

29. Carrying no offense.

30. Totally congruent having your deep inner thoughts aligned with heaven.

31. Living in great grace and favor.

Every one of these characteristics is true about you. God created you in such a way that these qualities will emerge in your life over time. You are in a process of transformation, and each characteristic is growing and gradually manifesting in you. They not only depict an accurate picture of who you are, but also each one is encouraging. Try standing in front of the mirror and say these out loud to yourself. Point to yourself and say, "God sees you as…." And go down the list. Believe me, you will feel like a new person.

ENDNOTES

[i] W. E. Vine, *An Expository Dictionary of Biblical Words* (Thomas Nelson Publishers, 1985), 524.

[ii] W. E. Vine, *An Expository Dictionary of Biblical Words* (Thomas Nelson Publishers, 1985), 639.

[iii] New Spirit Filled Life Bible, ed. Jack W. Hayford, Litt.D. (Thomas Nelson Publishers, 2002), 1675.

[iv] New Spirit Filled Life Bible, p. 1556.

About Linda

Linda Breitman—spiritual mother, mentor, and author of *Going Fishing: Practical Ways to Reach Your Neighbor*, is an ordained minister and international conference speaker. She has been a featured guest on the 700 Club and numerous radio and television programs. Linda grew up in San Jose and has lived all over the Northwestern United States. She and her husband settled in San Diego County in 1998. Since then, Linda has developed an intensified mentoring program with graduates who have moved on to become successful parents, business owners, ministry leaders, and missionaries. Linda currently holds Prophetic Intercession Training Schools, Dangerous Women Activation Seminars, and The Real You Identity Courses. She is passionate to see men and women rise up in their God given identities, becoming fully equipped to impact nations with a renewed mind and a supernatural lifestyle.

For more information about Linda Breitman, visit:
www.lindabreitman.com

Lets Connect...

 Facebook:
http://www.Facebook.com/Linda.Breitman

 Twitter: @LindaBreitman
http://www.Twitter.com/LindaBreitman

RESOURCES

THE REAL YOU
BELIEVING YOUR TRUE IDENTITY
CURRICULUM

Know what God says about you, believe in what He says, and activate it!

Featuring Seven Powerful Components:

- *The Real You: Believing Your True Identity*

- *The Real You Activation Manual*

- *The Real You Video Sessions*

- *The Real You Identity Decrees*

- *The Real You Identity Decrees CD*

- *The Real You Video Sessions for Leaders*

- *Soaking in Your True Identity CD*

These items can be purchased at:

LindaBreitman.com

CPSIA information can be obtained at www.ICGtesting.com
Printed in the USA
LVOW10s1114050514

384456LV00002B/263/P